Harvard University
Center for International Affairs

MIGRANTS, URBAN POVERTY, AND INSTABILITY IN DEVELOPING NATIONS

By *Joan M. Nelson*

OCCASIONAL PAPERS IN INTERNATIONAL AFFAIRS

Number 22

SEPTEMBER 1969

AMS PRESS
NEW YORK

Created in 1958, the Center for International Affairs fosters advanced study of basic world problems by scholars from various disciplines and senior officials from many countries. The research at the Center focuses on economic, social, and political development, the management of force in the modern world, and the evolving roles of Western Europe and the Communist bloc.

The Occasional Papers, which are listed on the inside back cover, may be ordered from the Publications Office, Center for International Affairs, 6 Divinity Avenue, Cambridge, Massachusetts 02138, at the prices indicated. Recent books written under the auspices of the Center, listed on the last page, may be obtained from bookstores or ordered direct from the publishers.

OCCASIONAL PAPERS IN INTERNATIONAL AFFAIRS

Number 22

SEPTEMBER 1969

MIGRANTS, URBAN POVERTY, AND INSTABILITY IN DEVELOPING NATIONS

By *Joan M. Nelson*

Published by the

Center for International Affairs

Harvard University

Cambridge, Mass.

1969

Library of Congress Cataloging in Publication Data

Nelson, Joan M
    Migrants, urban poverty, and instability in
developing nations.

    Original ed. issued as no. 22 of Occasional papers
in international affairs.
    Includes bibliographical references.
    1. Underdeveloped areas—Politics and government.
2. Radicalism. 3. Rural-urban migration. I. Title.
II. Series: Harvard University. Center for International Affairs. Occasional papers in international
affairs, no. 22.
[JF60.N45 1974]   320.9'172'4   74-9752
ISBN 0-404-54622-6

AMS PRESS INC.
NEW YORK, N. Y.   10003

ABOUT THE AUTHOR

Joan M. Nelson is Visiting Associate Professor, Department of Political Science, Massachusetts Institute of Technology, and Research Associate at the Center for International Affairs. In 1968-1969 she was also an International Affairs Fellow at the Council on Foreign Relations in New York City. Miss Nelson is the author of *Aid, Influence, and Foreign Policy* (New York: The Macmillan Co., 1968).

CONTENTS

TABLES

FIGURES

Foreword

There has been much speculation but little analysis of the political effects of rapid urban growth in the developing nations of Asia, Africa, and Latin America. The bulk of speculation and much of the small body of analysis have focussed on the question of political destabilization resulting from urbanization. This study criticizes two of the most frequently encountered theories of destabilization. In doing so, it draws on a variety of sources — attitude surveys, intensive studies of individual neighborhoods, employment and occupation samples, voting analyses, demographic studies and projections, historical analyses of the incidence of civil disturbances. Most of the data comes from those countries of the developing world which are comparatively urbanized or which have sizeable urban populations, including the major countries of Latin America and North Africa, as well as Turkey and India. However, material has been drawn from any situation which seemed relevant to the questions under consideration, including on specific points, nineteenth-century Europe and mid-twentieth-century Italy. Conversely, I have omitted material from sub-Saharan Africa and from those countries of Latin America and Asia where urbanization and industrialization are just getting under way. This eclectic and somewhat arbitrary approach is adequate to test the assumptions which underlie the standard destabilization theories, though it would not suffice for construction of alternative and better models.

I am grateful to the Center for International Affairs of Harvard University and to the Council on Foreign Relations for their financial support and intellectual stimulation during the period when this study was developed. Special thanks for thoughtful and constructive criticism of the monograph are due to Samuel P. Huntington, Frederick Frey, Don Horowitz, Abraham Lowenthal, and David Peirce. Gino Germani kindly provided unpublished data from his survey of mobility in Buenos Aires; Frank Bonilla permitted me to use data from CENDES survey print-out; Alex Inkeles generously provided access to the data from his modernization surveys; and Betsy Dunn of the Inkeles project patiently helped me locate the particular items I needed. I very much appreciate their assistance. Marina S. Finkelstein, Editor of Publications of the Center for International Affairs, guided the study to publication with skill and dispatch. Lois Fiore converted untidy manuscript and tables into orderly typescript with patience and good humor. To both, my thanks.

Joan M. Nelson

Cambridge, Massachusetts
May 1969.

INTRODUCTION

1. *Purpose*

Our image of the less developed world as predominantly rural and agricultural is only partly accurate, and grows steadily less so. Much of Asia and Africa are still largely rural. But a fifth to a third of the people of most Latin American countries live in cities of 100,000 or more. In Asia and North Africa, Lebanon, the U.A.R., and the Philippines are also substantially urbanized, and Morocco, Syria, Turkey, South Korea, and Taiwan are not far behind. Virtually everywhere in the developing world, regardless of the level of urbanization already achieved, cities are growing at rates of from 5 to 8 per cent annually. That is, they are doubling their populations every ten to fifteen years.[1]

The direct and indirect political repercussions of urban growth are far-reaching, but have been little explored. Among such implications are the political effects in rural areas and small towns of sustained out-migration by the more ambitious young adults; the direct political role of newcomers to the city; and the repercussions of urban growth and dislocation among longer-established urban groups, particularly the lower middle class. This study concentrates on only one of these topics: the political role of migrants to the larger cities, and more generally of the urban poor.

Why choose this focus? Quite simply because there is widespread anxiety among both foreign observers and the elite in the developing nations themselves that the swelling masses of urban poor will prove politically destabilizing. That is, they are expected to provide mass support for radical parties of the right or left (although the left is regarded as more probable), or to take to the streets, spontaneously or in response to agitation, so often and so violently as to cripple orderly administration and perhaps to topple governments.

[1]

This study will argue that such anxiety is ill-founded. Unlike organized labor, the lower strata of the urban working classes are usually politically passive. There is little evidence that they are generally resentful and frustrated, much less that they are likely to express such frustrations in the form of disruptive political behavior.

This is not to deny that in most developing nations, the cities are the centers of opposition to established governments, the loci of most radical movements, and the sites of sporadic demonstrations and political violence. They are also the home of the bulk of industry and higher education. Political protest initiated and dominated by labor unions, student leaders, or junior military officers is unlikely to involve the urban poor to any significant extent, unless special efforts have been made to encourage their participation. Similarly, rising support for extremist parties is not evidence of the radicalism of the poor, unless the votes can be traced explicitly to the lowest-income neighborhoods. In short, protest and instability fed by industrialization, the spread of higher education, and other processes which concentrate in cities should not be mistaken for turbulence resulting from the growth of the urban lower class.

Fear that the poor will be politically destabilizing has occasionally spurred ill-conceived, hasty, and partial housing and social programs which divert funds and effort from the long-range, realistic planning necessary to cope with their problems. Scholars have also been preoccupied with destabilization, and have largely ignored other important questions about the political role of the urban poor in the developing nations. To disprove, or at least to cast serious doubt on theories of destabilization may therefore contribute both to sounder policy and more fruitful research.

Laying to rest the theories that migrants and the urban poor are politically disruptive leaves open two broader questions. First, what groups are in fact the sources of urban violence and extremism? Second, what political role, if any, may we expect migrants and the poor in general to play under varying circumstances?

A number of scholars have analyzed the roots of civil disorder in developing societies. Some have taken a quantitative cross-national approach, attempting to link various kinds of dis-

[2]

turbances with broad economic, social, and political characteristics and trends.[2] Such studies do not identify the specific groups most involved in unrest, except by inference. For example, a large number of strikes suggests that organized labor is a leading protest group, though other groups may also be involved. Analyses of individual countries seldom take civil unrest as a central focus,[3] but such studies inevitably discuss important protest incidents. They usually identify the groups most heavily involved as students, labor unions, the military, and alienated elites. This monograph does not attempt to probe beyond such studies, except in the sense that it affirms they have not overlooked any major contributor to disorder in the form of the urban lower classes.

The actual and potential political roles of the urban poor have received much less scholarly attention than the sources of civic disorder. The present study does not explore this question, but it does attempt to clear the way for such exploration. It is essentially a site-clearing operation, designed to tear down two flimsy structures which have blocked construction of a sounder and more ample theory of the role of migrants and the urban poor. The task of construction itself is much more ambitious, and beyond the scope of this monograph.

2. Background

Before turning to a close examination of the two most common destabilization theories, a brief review of the background facts is in order. The basic point can be stated briefly: in much of the developing world, the urban labor force is growing much more rapidly than the supply of urban jobs for unskilled and semi-skilled workers. Public health and sanitation measures have cut mortality in the cities while birthrates remain high, producing rapid rates of natural population increase. Added to this is the steady flow of migrants from rural areas and provincial towns. In many countries, migration reflects population pressure on the land, in turn the result of improved rural health services and famine-averting transportation networks. Even where land is plentiful, however, people stream to the cities. The very processes which promote rural modernization and integration — education, mass media, transportation — also spur the exodus in search of a better life. Those who go are, disproportionately, young adults just entering or recently having entered the labor market.

While the urban labor supply mushrooms, the number of well-paid and secure manual jobs expands painfully slowly. Modern manufacturing is the source which comes most readily to mind. But in many developing countries, manufacturing is expanding rather slowly, often from a very low base. And regardless of the rate of expansion, much new investment is in relatively capital-intensive enterprises. Modern technology is labor-saving. Moreover, social and legal factors often raise the cost of labor and reduce the cost of capital to entrepreneurs.[4] Maintenance considerations and availability of spare parts discourage use of older and more labor-intensive technology. In state-owned enterprises, nationalist pride works in the same direction. Outside of manufacturing, good low-level employment opportunities exist in modern segments of transportation, communications, and power, and in larger and more modern public and private service enterprises. But these sources expand slowly. As a result, more and more urban workers are forced into jobs which produce and pay little and offer limited or no security — unskilled construction work, jobs as assistants or apprentices in artisan manufacturing, domestic service, petty vending, loading and carrying, shoe-shining, scrap collecting.

Reported rates of open unemployment are high but not appalling in most large cities of the developing world.[5] Rates of from 5 to 10 per cent appear repeatedly in surveys of major Latin American and Indian cities. However, rates among the unskilled, and among young men looking for their first job are far higher. Unemployment is also more extensive in the major cities than in smaller ones. In India, for example, rates in Bombay, Calcutta, Madras, and Delhi were from 50 to 100 per cent higher than in cities of less than 300,000.[6]

Urban underemployment must greatly exceed unemployment, but it is extremely difficult to measure. A proxy indicator of the extent of underemployment is productivity in the tertiary or service sector, which drops as the sector is swollen by peddling, domestic service, and other marginal occupations. It has been calculated that in Latin America between 1950 and 1965, while productivity in agriculture grew at 1.8 per cent a year and industry, mining, and utilities gained 2.5 per cent annually, productivity in the service sectors fell, suggesting "a level of underemployment equivalent to 10 per cent of the national labor force."[7] Since services absorb much more urban than rural labor, the implied underemployment rate in the cities would far exceed 10 per cent.

Many worried analysts and policy-makers conclude that rapid growth in much of the developing world does not operate as an engine of economic progress, transferring workers from low-productivity farm work to more productive and remunerative urban jobs. Rather, it is largely a process of geographic redistribution, shifting poverty from the countryside to the cities.[8]

In Latin America, the growing numbers of unskilled, semi-employed, and abysmally poor urbanites are often called the "marginals." The term is apt. The people to whom it is applied are economically marginal, in that they contribute little to and benefit little from production and economic growth. Their social status is low, and they are excluded from the formal organizations and associations and the informal and private webs of contacts which constitute the urban social structure. To the extent that they are rural in origin, they may also be culturally marginal, clinging to customs, manners, dress, speech, and values which contrast with accepted urban patterns. They lack ties to or influence on the established political institutions. Many are marginal in a literal geographic sense, living in squatter settlements on the fringes of the cities.[9] All this, of course, is from the point of view of established metropolitan and national elites. To what degree and in what respects the urban poor regard themselves as marginal remains an open question.

Against this background, prophesies of chaos and revolution take two main forms.[10] Some of the prophets focus on the migrants. Uprooted, isolated, disappointed, and frustrated, they are viewed as tinder for any demagogic or extremist spark. Others argue just the opposite: new migrants are politically passive. The threat to stability lies not with the newcomers, but with those deprived and frustrated slum and shanty dwellers who are longer urban residents, or with the second generation. These contentions are explored in turn.

[5]

CHAPTER I

THE DISRUPTIVE MIGRANTS

All over the world, often long in advance of effective industrialization, the unskilled poor are streaming away from subsistence
agriculture to exchange the squalor of rural poverty for the even
deeper miseries of the shantytowns, favelas, and bidonvilles that,
year by year, grow inexorably on the fringes of the developing
cities. They . . . are the core of local despair and disaffection—
filling the Jeunesse movements of the Congo, swelling the urban
mobs of Rio, voting Communist in the ghastly alleys of Calcutta,
everywhere undermining the all too frail structure of public order
and thus retarding the economic development that alone can help
their plight.[1]

Barbara Ward

The men whom the growing population of the country districts
and colonial expropriation have brought to desert their family
holdings circle tirelessly around the different towns, hoping that
one day or another they will be allowed inside. . . . For the
lumpen-proletariat, that horde of starving men, uprooted from
their tribe and from their clan, constitutes one of the most spon-
taneous and the most radically revolutionary forces of a colonized
people.[2]

Frantz Fanon

In cities growing at annual rates of 5 per cent or more,
natural population growth accounts for roughly a third to a half
of the increase. Migration from other cities, towns, and rural
areas makes up the remainder. At such rates, migrants[3] come
to constitute the bulk of the urban population within a few decades. Many of the migrants are very recently arrived. For
example, a 1959 survey of six large Brazilian cities found that 75
per cent of the adult population sampled had been born outside
of the cities where they were interviewed. Twenty-seven per
cent had arrived within the previous decade.[4] In 1964, slightly
more than half of Bogotá's 1.7 million people had been born
outside its metropolitan limits. More than a third of the city's
population had migrated within the preceding eleven years and
almost a quarter had arrived in the last five years.[5]

1. *The Theory*

Many observers believe that this immense influx of migrants
is a major source of urban instability. Their predictions rest on
several apparently reasonable assumptions.

[6]

Migrants are assumed to be uprooted, isolated, and therefore anomic, that is, unrestrained by binding norms of behavior. In rural areas, established institutions and relations of centuries guide political attitudes and action, instilling habits of deference and passivity. Migrants are uprooted from this setting and plunged into a bewildering, harsh, impersonal environment where traditional controls are absent or irrelevant, while effective alternative forms of control have not been established or are not recognized. Philip Hauser, among others, sets forth this line of reasoning:

> The acute as well as chronic aspects of social problems that result from rapid urbanization are, perhaps, most discernible in the adjustment of migrants to urban living. The rural in-migrant to the city is typically from a relatively homogeneous origin. In the city, he is confronted with a bewildering and almost incomprehensible vastness and heterogeneity. He usually lives for some time with his fellow villagers or relatives and only gradually becomes accommodated to city life. He must adapt to new and unfamiliar ways of making a living; a money economy; regular working hours; the absence of warm family living; large numbers of impersonal contacts with other human beings; new forms of recreation; and a quite different physical setting, often involving new kinds of housing, sanitation, traffic congestion, and noise. . . . In such a setting, the in-migrant frequently displays personal disorganization as the subjective aspect of social disorganization.[6]

Or, more concisely, Soares and Hamblin:

> Anomie ordinarily occurs . . . when people migrate from home, and particularly when they move to cities.[7]

Beyond uprootedness and anomie, the migrant is often assumed to be disappointed and frustrated. He has moved to the city to escape grinding rural poverty. But the city offers only low-wage, insecure employment for the unskilled. He must move in with already over-crowded relatives, find a tenement room, or locate a dilapidated shack in a brawling, filthy shantytown. At the same time that his vision of his own future is shattered, he sees in streets and store windows undreamed-of luxuries. Small wonder, then, if he becomes disillusioned, bitter, readily persuaded to political violence or extremism.

2. *The Evidence*

If this reasoning is valid, we would expect to find propor-

[7]

tionately more recent migrants than either established migrants or urban-born supporting extremist parties or taking part in demonstrations and riots. Unfortunately, the few studies which come closest to testing the hypothesis do not distinguish between more and less recent arrivals, but treat all migrants as a single category. Nonetheless, the studies are striking in that they all tend to refute the hypothesis.

Myron Weiner has used voting and demographic data from Calcutta to test the voting tendencies of migrants to that city. Indian migration typically includes a high proportion of single men and men leaving their families in their home villages while they seek work in the cities. Districts in Calcutta with high ratios of men to women may therefore be assumed to include high proportions of migrants. Using voting data from the 1957 and 1962 elections for state assemblymen, Weiner found that the rank order correlation between sex ratios by constituency and the proportion of voters in those constituencies who supported the Congress Party approached .80 in both elections. Third factors such as voting turn-out, literacy, and the number of slum-dwellers in the constituency did not seem to affect the remarkably high relationship. Since the Congress Party is viewed in Calcutta as moderate to conservative, there is a strong inference that migrants were more moderate in their party preferences than the city electorate as a whole.[8]

Glaucio Soares and Robert Hamblin explored the relation between migration, among other socio-economic variables, and radicalism on a country-wide basis for Chile. They found a negative relation between the proportion of migrants to total population in each of the twenty-five departments or states of Chile, and the proportion of the total valid vote supporting Socialist Party candidate Salvador Allende Gossens in the 1952 presidential elections.[9] While data for entire departments may mask contrary tendencies within each department, nonetheless the Chilean statistics cast doubt on the hypothesis that migrants vote disproportionately for radical or extremist candidates.

Perhaps, however, radicalism is the wrong index. Political protest in the form of a radical vote is somewhat sophisticated. Newer migrants may be systematically disenfranchised by residence requirements. Moreover, there are not always radical parties, or for that matter elections, through which to express frustration. Anomie and bitterness might appear more simply and directly in the form of turmoil and politically motivated violence.

If it is difficult to locate evidence on precisely how migrants vote, it is still harder to identify those who took part in riots and demonstrations. The only studies along such lines which I have been able to locate draw on contemporary United States and nineteenth-century French data rather than on data from the developing nations. The findings of the President's Commission on Civil Disorders regarding the ghetto riots of the summer of 1967 in the United States are nonetheless suggestive.

> Both survey data and arrest records demonstrate unequivocally that those brought up in the region in which the riot occurred are much more likely to have participated in the riots. The percentage of rioters brought up in the North is almost identical for the Detroit survey—74.4 percent—and the Newark survey—74.0 percent. By contrast, of the non-involved, 36.0 percent in Detroit and 52.4 percent in Newark were brought up in the North. . . . Rioters are not only more likely than the non-involved to have been born in the North, but they are also more likely to have been long-term residents of the city in which the disturbances took place.[10]

Peter Lupsha cites additional studies of recent U.S. riots, all of which find migrants relatively uninvolved.[11] Comparisons between contemporary U.S. urban ghettoes and the slums and squatter settlements of cities in developing countries are suspect. The situations differ in many important ways. However, by the standards of the underdeveloped world, black Americans in the rural south have relatively high access to education and media exposure. The gap in political information and sophistication between northern urban and southern rural blacks is probably narrower than that between rural farmhands and urban manual workers in most developing countries. In the context of American race relations and the political climate of the late 1960's, one might expect a greater tendency to political activism and perhaps to violence among American blacks recently arrived in city ghettoes than among rural migrants elsewhere. Therefore, the finding that in fact they are underrepresented among urban rioters might be expected to apply still more strongly abroad.

Urbanization, industrialization, and urban violence in nineteenth-century France led contemporaries and later historians to

[9]

theories similar to those propounded today about Latin America, Africa, and Asia. For example, Louis Chevalier, writing of the Restoration and the July Monarchy, asserts:

> Beyond the conflict of classes and independently of the development of class consciousness, a purely Parisian problem was being settled during these years: the problem of a population seeking a place in a hostile setting and then, having failed, turning to every sort of hatred, of violence, of violation.[12]

Yet Charles Tilly points out that the relation between voluminous migration, rapid urban growth, and political upheaval is tenuous at best.

> Although people were moving to the cities and urban population was expanding vigorously from the restoration into the early years of the Third Republic, the peaks were the later 1850's and the later 1870's, hardly major moments for political disturbances. In fact (if we wanted to pay any attention at all to this sort of curve-fitting) it would be easier to argue that stepped-up cityward migration and urban growth *followed* major upheavals than vice versa.[13]

Looking more closely at the geographic distribution of urban growth and of violence, Tilly and his associates find no consistent relationship at all between the frequency of violent conflicts in a department and the current rate of increase in the urban population for the years between 1821 and 1866.

> While it is true that fast-growing Paris, Nantes, Bordeaux, Lyon and their departments were exceptionally turbulent in the 1830's, so were slow-moving Nîmes, Grenoble, and Auxerre. Conversely, Marseille, Toulouse, Saint-Etienne and several of the other leaders experienced rather little violent conflict during the period. Even Paris underwent its greatest growth (especially its growth through migration) just *after* the July Revolution and *after* Louis Napoleon's seizure of power.[14]

3. Where the Theory Goes Wrong

Scattered evidence on current political behavior, historical material, and survey data converge, then, to suggest that rural-to-urban migrants are not politically disruptive. Data which can explain where the theory goes wrong are more plentiful than evidence on the behavior itself. The assumption that migrants, particularly newcomers, tend to be politically destabilizing rests on the image of such migrants as uprooted, isolated, and de-

[10]

prived, hence anomic, frustrated, and prone to express frustration through political channels. Each aspect of this image can be separately examined.

Uprootedness and anomie. First, although migrants are by definition uprooted, they may be better prepared for big-city life than is commonly assumed. By far the most important point to note is that much migration into the great cities comes from smaller cities and towns rather than from open country. The proportions vary greatly from country to country and among major cities within each country. But illustrative data may be of interest:

—In Santiago, Chile, two-thirds of a sample of economically active migrants were born in towns of 10,000 or over. Only a seventh had been born in places of less than 1,000. The town-dwellers' share in total migration into Santiago is much higher than a random sample of the total population would produce.[15]

—Among migrants to six Brazilian cities (excluding immigrants from abroad), 23 per cent came from other large cities, 56 per cent said their place of origin was a small city or town, and 21 per cent were from clearly rural places.[16]

These figures reflect the increasingly well-documented pattern of step-migration, with rural migrants often moving not to the nearest large city but to a provincial town. Later they or their children may move on to a larger city.

In India, where 75 per cent of the population still lives in villages of less than 2,000 population, the strong rural preponderance heightens the probability that many migrants into even the largest cities will come directly from the countryside.

—In Bombay, a little over one-fifth of migrants entering since 1941 (excluding refugees from Pakistan) came from other towns and cities. The proportion of migrants from urban areas has been increasing: among the most recent arrivals, a quarter are of urban origin.[17]

—In Delhi, only half of the migrants (excluding refugees) are of rural origin.[18] The substantial number of migrants from other cities, many of professional or managerial back-

[11]

ground, undoubtedly results in part from the large proportion of the labor force concentrated in government jobs.

Those migrants who do jump directly from farm to metropolitan center tend to come from not too distant villages. In a
largely migrant working class *barrio* in Bogotá, 60 per cent of the
migrants were from rural areas. Two-thirds of those in the
sample had travelled less than one hundred miles to settle in
Bogotá.[19] In a similar settlement on the edge of Ankara, Turkey,
77 per cent of those surveyed had come from villages, and two-
thirds had travelled less than one hundred twenty-five miles.[20]
Herrick, analyzing migration to Santiago, Chile, found that the
bulk of the migrants came from the central third of the country,
where much of the population is concentrated. Within this central region, "the effect of distance as a discouraging factor to
migration was surprisingly linear."[21]

Villages and towns not too far from major metropolitan
centers are likely to be heavily exposed to mass media, government activity, urban consumer goods, and other urban influences.
Moreover, those who move to the city from nearby villages are
likely to maintain ties with friends and relatives left behind, and
to return for visits on family occasions and holidays,[22] thereby
both re-inforcing their own rural ties and introducing urban influences to the village. Many of those who make the big move
have also visited urban friends or relatives once or several times
before deciding to settle permanently in the city. In some cases
moving to the city may be a common, almost an expected,
pattern in the migrant's home town. Mario Margulis describes
such a pattern in the isolated Argentinian town of Chilecito,
from which many young men and women regularly departed
for the capital and other cities.[23] Similarly, the town of Kara-
koy, Turkey, encourages its young men to seek work in Ankara,
some fifty miles away.

> From childhood they were acquainted with conditions in Ankara
> and those coffee houses or shops where they were likely to en-
> counter helpful kinsmen. Karakoy women were not considered
> near-prostitutes if they became domestic servants. In fact, their
> marriage value might be improved if they could demonstrate an
> ability to add to the family coffers. Even young boys frequently
> were placed in homes of wealthy families of Ankara to perform
> household chores and gain an urban "polish."[24]

[12]

Anthony and Elizabeth Leeds carry this line of thought a step farther, and argue that even small towns and *latifundia* far from major cities may provide experience which prepares the potential migrant for adjustment to urban life. Many farm workers have experience with selling and buying in cash markets, and some offer services like barbering as a sideline. Such migrants are:

> . . . familiar with modalities of transactions, with the urban ambience, with the urban institutions—police, bureaucrats, licensing, trade, exchange, traffic flow, transportation, etc. [They do] not come unknowing and unprepared for large city life.

Moreover, the Leeds suggest, "peasant shrewdness" and other values and practices may be highly adaptive in urban settings.[25]

Pre-migration exposure to urban life styles, either through the penetration of urban influences into village life or through visits to the city, must substantially reduce the cultural shock felt by many new migrants. This observation cuts two ways with respect to their political behavior. Those who are better prepared for urban life are also likely to become politically active, though not necessarily politically disruptive, earlier than their less sophisticated fellow-migrants. Some may even become radical or violent. But if they do so, it is for quite different reasons than the cultural shock and anomie assumed in the theory under examination.

The theory of the anomic and potentially disruptive migrant assumes not only that most migrants have little prior contact with urban ways, but also that they come, for the most part, from tightly structured families and communities with stable and clearly defined norms and patterns of relationships. This is probably true in large parts of South Asia and Africa. In Latin America, however, an increasing proportion of the rural population are migratory landless laborers, squatters, or pioneer cultivators with few if any local ties.

> . . . [R]ecent evidence points to an unexpected prominence of individualism and internal conflict even within the apparently tightly-knit local groups found mainly among the Indians, and confirms that local cohesion is weak or lacking in much of the region. Meanwhile, the growth, increasing geographic mobility and increasing involvement with national life of the rural population have produced new strains on the traditional forms, and alto-

gether detached an important part of the rural population from their influence.[26]

These trends have little to do with affirmative preparation for adjustment to urban life. But they do undercut the assumption of trauma resulting from the shattering of deeply ingrained norms, values, and relationships.

Social isolation and anomie. The degree of social isolation new migrants suffer may also be exaggerated. Most newcomers undoubtedly have fewer friends and more limited contacts in the city than more established residents. Gino Germani's comparison of two adjacent working class neighborhoods in Buenos Aires, one composed largely of recent migrants and the other more settled, documents the newcomers' relative isolation.[27] However, the great majority of migrants do have contacts in the city when they arrive. Among the recent migrants Germani surveyed in Buenos Aires, 81 per cent found friends or relatives or both upon arrival, and 60 per cent received assistance in finding housing, work, or money to tide them over the first days.[28] Two separate surveys of migrants in Santiago, Chile, found that 83 per cent had friends or family in the city or received assistance in settling.[29] Ninety-two per cent of the migrants in a Bogotá squatter settlement had contacts on arrival;[30] the same was true of three-quarters of the migrants in the Brazilian six-city survey.[31] Home-town associations in some Latin American[32] and North African countries, tribal and home-town associations in the cities of Western and Central Africa, and caste associations in many Indian cities also offer contacts, advice, and psychological support to new arrivals.

Despite previous urban exposure, friends and relatives, and the possibility of club affiliations, many newcomers undoubtedly do feel more or less uprooted and isolated. My point is merely that our picture of their plight should not be overdrawn. More specifically, assumptions of acute unhappiness and personal and social disorganization probably are not warranted. Government housing corporation (CORVI) social workers in Santiago did not find that migrants faced special problems different from those of others in their social and economic circumstances.[33] Richard Patch described a great deal of personal and social disorganization in the center city slums of Lima,[34] but William Mangin and Jerome Cohen found little support in the course of extensive ob-

[14]

servation and varied psychological testing in Lima lower-class neighborhoods, for the suggestion that the trauma of migration produces serious disturbance or mental illness.[35] Most migrants are young adults, and there is some evidence that many of them are better educated and trained than the average in their places of origin. These facts undoubtedly contribute to their desire and capacity to adjust to urban life.

Dissatisfaction with economic conditions. The third assumption regarding migrants — that they are disappointed and frustrated by economic conditions in the city — is not merely modified but contradicted by the evidence. Survey findings are virtually unanimous on the point that most migrants consider themselves better off, and probably are in fact better off, than they were before they moved. In view of conditions in the city, this is a shocking testimonial to even worse conditions in the countryside, but the point is none the less relevant.

Looking first at employment, most migrants seem to find jobs fairly quickly. (See Table 1.) The high proportions finding

Table 1

Time Required for Migrants to Find First Job in City

City	Sample	Per Cent Finding Work	Within:
Santiago, Chile[37]	310 economically active migrants arriving in Santiago within previous decade. Roughly 40 per cent white collar.	40 per cent	2 days
		63 per cent	1 month
		80 per cent	6 months
Santiago, Chile[38]	276 family heads or their wives in a *callampa* settlement; 85 per cent manual laborers or self-employed artisans.	47 per cent	"immediately"
		91 per cent	3 months
Buenos Aires[39]	446 residents of a *villa miseria*, mostly recent migrants, 61 per cent day laborers or unskilled workers.	74 per cent	2 weeks
		85 per cent	1 month
Brazil: six cities[40] (includes Rio and São Paulo)	5250 adults, including 3035 migrants of whom 1483 sought jobs on arrival.	80 per cent	1 month
		95 per cent (male) 90 per cent (female) }	4 mos.

[15]

work almost immediately suggest that many migrants have jobs lined up before they arrive.[36]

Surveys consistently show lower rates of open unemployment among migrants than among native urbanites. This is true for city-wide or more limited surveys in Bogotá,[41] Santiago,[42] Calcutta,[43] Delhi,[44] Bombay,[45] Lucknow,[46] and Karachi.[47] Are migrants simply more willing to take ill-paid, insecure jobs? This may apply to unskilled migrants, many of whom come from rural areas. In his samples of working class groups in Buenos Aires, Germani found that recently arrived male migrants were ten times more likely than urban-born men to be unskilled (61 per cent, compared to 6 per cent). Less than half of the recent migrants worked throughout the year; a third could find employment for only six months or less.[48] In Delhi, migrants comprised 45 per cent of the casual day laborers, but only 32 per cent of the labor force as a whole.[49] In Santiago, migrants, and especially migrant women, were more heavily concentrated in personal service occupations than were the native-born.[50]

Although those migrants who are unskilled may avoid unemployment only by accepting marginal jobs, the occupation patterns for all migrants taken as a group do not differ markedly from the occupational distribution among the urban-born. Samples based on cross-sections of the entire labor force in Santiago and Bombay found little difference between the occupation distributions of migrants and natives.[51] In Lucknow in the mid-1950's, migrants were over-represented among holders of high-pay, high-prestige jobs. Twenty-six per cent of migrants, compared to 15 per cent of the natives, held managerial, professional, and lower-level administrative and executive positions. More generally, 63 per cent of the migrants and only 37 per cent of the natives were salaried; at the other end of the scale, 11 per cent of the migrants and 16 per cent of the natives were casual or daily workers.[52] In Delhi also, in the mid-1950's, more migrants than urban-born held higher-level occupations.[53]

Lower rates of open unemployment among migrants may partly reflect different age distributions among migrant and native populations. Even though most migrants are young adults when they arrive, where migration has continued for some years the mean age of migrants is likely to be higher than that of natives, many of whom are the children of early migrants.[54] Un-

[16]

employment is everywhere disproportionately high among adolescents and those in their early twenties. The higher proportion of people in these age brackets among the native-born would tend to swell unemployment rates for urbanites as a whole. Different age distributions may also have some effect on the differences in occupational distributions between migrants and native-born.

More broadly, the data on employment rates and patterns highlight the risks of regarding all migrants as an undifferentiated, low-level group. The surprising statistics do not really invalidate the widespread impression that many migrants arrive untrained and ill-prepared, and must struggle to survive from day-to-day on odd jobs. However, the figures do underscore the fact that many other migrants, probably including large numbers from towns and smaller cities, bring to the great metropolitan centers skills and education as good or better than the average for those centers. Not surprisingly, these migrants do quite well.

From the standpoint of the migrants' satisfaction, it is less important to determine how their occupations compare with those of natives than whether they have improved their situations by moving. Delhi offers the most clear-cut information, although experience there may reflect special factors which apply weakly or not at all to other cases. Among those migrants to Delhi who were employed before moving to the Indian capital, 46 per cent had held "subordinate technical" (manual) jobs, while at the time of the survey only 18 per cent held such positions. Proportions in transportation jumped from 7 to 18 per cent, those in ministerial (mostly clerical) jobs from 10 to 16 per cent, and those in "subordinate administrative and executive" positions doubled from 9 to 18 per cent. Before moving, 25 per cent earned more than 100 rupees monthly. At the time of the survey, 41 per cent earned at least 100 rupees; most of those with increased incomes now earned between 100 and 250 rupees per month.[55] Herrick offers only fragmentary information of a comparable kind for Santiago migrants; he found that 18 per cent of the men in his sample had held white-collar jobs before moving, while 35 per cent held such jobs at the time of the survey.[56]

Bertram Hutchinson has compared the jobs of migrants in six Brazilian cities to their fathers' most recent occupations, rather than to their own jobs prior to migration. Of 1,182 adult male

[17]

migrants, 39 per cent held positions higher than their fathers'; 43 per cent held jobs classified as having equal status; and 18 per cent had dropped below their fathers' status. Hutchinson's data also suggest that rural migrants are least likely to have risen above their fathers' status, while migrants from other large cities are most likely to have done so.[57] In other words, migrants who were unskilled rural laborers in all probability remain unskilled as urban workers.

This does not mean that they have failed to improve their lot, at least in their own view. Sixty-one per cent of the men in Germani's sample of recent migrants were unskilled or day laborers. Eleven per cent were skilled, and 11 per cent held white collar jobs. As a group, they were less satisfied with their jobs than were the better-established migrants and urban-born. But almost all of them viewed working conditions in the city as an improvement over their previous situation.[58] Hutchinson found low job turnover among Brazilian migrants. In São Paulo, for example, migrants had spent an average of twenty years when interviewed, and had held an average of slightly fewer than three jobs.[59] Admittedly, this is an ambiguous yardstick which may reflect resignation in the face of a tight job market rather than real job satisfaction. But São Paulo has probably offered wider job opportunities than most cities in the developing world. Studies of factory workers (a small and privileged fraction of the urban labor force in general and a still smaller proportion of migrants) concur that the workers prefer factory to field work, both because it is easier and because it carries more prestige.[60] Guillermo Briones distinguished more and less recent migrants in his sample of Lima factory workers, and found that the most recent migrants were the most satisfied.[61]

Although this evidence is fragmentary, it seems to indicate consistently for a number of cities that most migrants who seek employment find it reasonably quickly. Moreover, the great majority find their new work an improvement over their positions before moving, in terms of working conditions and, less uniformly, status and earnings.

Satisfaction with housing probably varies widely, not only with the adequacy of urban housing (and the climate, which largely determines what is adequate), but also with the standards to which migrants are accustomed before moving. In Germani's

[18]

Buenos Aires sample most migrants felt that they had had better housing in their home towns or villages. But half of these migrants had come from large towns.[62] On a cross-national scale they were probably comparatively privileged. Both Pearse[63] and Bonilla[64] have remarked that *favela* housing in urban Brazil is much the same as rural housing throughout the nation.

> What is significant, however, and what is overlooked constantly by the city commentators who weep over the favelas, is that though the house-type is "rural," the conditions of life which the favela dwellers—by their illegal initiative (in building squatter settlements)—have secured for themselves, are rated higher by them in most respects than the conditions prevailing in the rural areas from which the greater number of them have come.[65]

In Asima, a squalid fringe settlement outside of Baghdad where the bulk of the residents come from extremely poor rural areas, housing consists of reed-matting shacks with mud-plaster roofs, entirely without plumbing and sparsely supplied with outdoor water taps. Yet three-quarters of a sample of 1,360 persons in Asima concurred that their housing was an improvement over their previous accommodations.[66]

While concrete employment and living conditions relative to previous experience and expectations are undoubtedly the prime determinants of migrants' satisfaction or dissatisfaction, intangibles may add to their sense of relative well-being. The city offers entertainment, formal and informal. It offers information, and the status which urban residence in itself confers. Perhaps most important, people who move to the city believe that their children will have more opportunity for education and advancement than they would have in rural areas or small towns —a judgment with which few could quarrel, however slim the chances of advancement in the city.

For many reasons, then, most migrants feel they have gained by moving. Eighty per cent of the Asima sample believed their total incomes, in cash and kind, were higher, and 90 per cent viewed their present diets as an improvement. Almost every family owned a kerosene cooking stove, an immense advance over brush and dung fires.[67] In *Barrio El Carmen* on the edge of Bogotá, a squatter settlement improved to the point where three-fourths of the houses were one- or two-story brick with sheet metal roofs; "the overwhelming majority . . . stated that their housing, sanitation facilities, income, medical service, and educational opportunities for the children were better in the barrio than in their previous countryside residences. Few expressed any desire to return to their area of origin."[68] A survey among squatters in Ankara, Turkey, found that 42 per cent described city life as more comfortable, 19 per cent cited more work and money, 8 per cent mentioned better health conditions, 3 per cent referred to more entertainment, while 2 per cent believed that they were better off in their home villages, and 17 per cent claimed no difference in living conditions.[69] Janet Abu-Lughod, discussing urban growth in the U.A.R., concludes:

> Only a naive romantic could claim that the plight of the urban proletariat of Egypt is not superior to that of the landless and hopeless rural family that turns in desperation to city life.[70]

The many migrants who come from smaller cities and towns rather than from the countryside undoubtedly have higher standards, but are also likely to do better in the city.

Venting frustration through political channels. Although most migrants feel better off, undoubtedly some are disappointed and bitter. However, there is little reason to expect those who are embittered to express their frustration politically. In Asia and sub-Saharan Africa, back-migration provides a safety valve for the disappointed. In these regions, many migrants are married men who leave their families in their home village. They plan to send money back to them, and may bring them to the city if things go well. However, if they fail to find adequate jobs, or if a depression forces them out of work, it is not difficult to return home. In Ankara, a *geçekondu* resident who loses his job "will generally lock his house and return to the village after several weeks unless another job can be found."[71] In Latin America, back-migration may be more difficult. Many migrants are single men or women; many others move as family units to the city. They are less likely to leave an established family base in their home town or village to which they can return if necessary.

Those who are disappointed but cannot or will not flee the city can express their frustration in an infinite variety of ways. They may turn their anger inward in withdrawal and defeat; they may beat their wives or quarrel with their neighbors; they may seek oblivion in alcohol or solace in religion.[72]   In addition to these individual reactions, there are many associational responses with little or no political relevance.   Political action, whether individual or associational, moderate or extremist, legal or illegal, is only one class of reactions to frustration among many others. The point is obvious, yet it is often overlooked.

Moreover, the more recent a migrant's arrival in the city, the less likely he is to translate frustration over economic conditions (or any other problem) into political action.   Those migrants who come directly from rural areas are likely to have little political interest or awareness, and may bring with them ingrained attitudes of fatalism and habits of deference to authority.   In many countries, these general orientations are re-enforced by political loyalty to or habits of voting for moderate or conservative parties. Such parties dominate much of rural Latin America, Asia, and North Africa, although radical parties in some countries are now seriously trying to penetrate the countryside.   Myron Weiner traces migrant support for Congress candidates in Calcutta in part to long-established Congress Party control of the rural areas from which the migrants come.[73]   However, heavy rural votes for conservative or moderate candidates may often reflect a network of patron-client relationships or other aspects of rural social organization rather than voter commitment.   In this context, migrants' party allegiances may be unstable once they move away from the social setting which enforced loyalty.

It is more difficult to generalize about the political backgrounds of those many migrants who come from towns and provincial cities, rather than rural areas.   It is a fair guess that they are more politically alert and less deferential than their rural counterparts.   More information on political patterns and ambience in towns and small cities in specific countries would be an important contribution to our understanding of migrants' political behavior in the major metropolitan centers.

The probability that recent migrants will choose political means of expressing such dissatisfaction as they may feel is affected not only by the political attitudes and habits they bring with them, but also by the political influences to which they are exposed in the city.   Recent Italian experience, which contrasts sharply with that in Latin America and Asia, illustrates both points particularly clearly.[74]

[21]

Between 1945 and 1964 an estimated four million southern peasants, mostly from central and southern Italy, moved to northern Italian cities. In 1951, 42 per cent of the entire Italian labor force was in agriculture; a decade later only 32 per cent remained so engaged, and by 1963 the proportion of the labor force in agriculture had dropped to 25 per cent.[75]

In this same period, Communist votes in northern cities have risen substantially.

> The great bulk of the immigrants . . . vote for the Communists. Between the general elections of 1958 and the local elections of 1964, there was an increase of 276,723 in the number of valid votes in the province of Rome. In that period the Communists gained 127,426 votes, while the Christian Democrats actually lost 9,831 votes. . . .
>
> The six provinces in which the Communists made their greatest gain in absolute number of votes between 1958 and 1963 were the same provinces—Milan, Turin, Rome, Florence, Genoa, and Bologna—in which there had been the greatest increases in population due to immigration. . . .[76]

These data suggest, without proving, that many migrants vote Communist. There is harder evidence that migrants have been in the vanguard of urban demonstrations and riots.

> Inherent in the urbanization process is also a certain potential for anomic movements, rioting, and disorder. Of the thousand people arrested in Turin during the riots of the summer of 1962, over two-thirds were southern immigrants, most of them very young, many of them barely able to speak Italian.[77]

Radical and violent behavior on the part of Italian migrants is an intriguing contrast to migrants' behavior elsewhere. A closer look at the forces shaping their behavior illuminates the earlier argument rather than invalidating it, and highlights the importance of the political context.

In general, Italian rural areas, like those in most modernizing countries and indeed throughout the world, tend to be conservative. "There is a regular increase in Catholic voting as one leaves the large urban centers for the smaller villages."[78] However, in the central Italian regions of Lombardy, Tuscany, and Emilia, where the Church was both government and major landholder in the eighteenth century, anti-clericalism is strong and widespread. "These areas of central Italy have voted for the

Left since pre-Fascist times, and are among the 'reddest' zones of Western Europe."[79]   Thus some migrants' communism is a simple transfer of old loyalties to new settings.   "The rebellious, pioneering, activistic temperament associated with rural Communist voting in the South also produces migration to the North."[80] The disposition to resort to violence also seems to be in part a carry-over of rural patterns.

> There are strong cultural differences between northern and southern Communists.   Southern Communists are typically bewildered by the behavior of their northern comrades.   They cannot understand the way in which things are discussed in local party sections: the problems seem unreal and the language difficult to fathom for those who bring their shotguns north with them, together with fresh memories of violence at home.[81]

But the move to the city has also led many who previously voted Christian Democrat or even Monarchist or neo-Fascist to support the Communist party.   Fried cites six causes of conversion.   Two are the familiar arguments of "liberation from the social controls of the village" and "protest against discrimination, exploitation, and squalor."   Evidence from other rapidly urbanizing nations suggests that these alone are inadequate to account for the observed behavior.   And it may not be wholly coincidental that Fried does not offer evidence or elaboration of these two points, but seems to take them as self-evident.   His discussion concentrates on four additional factors: "anxiety to adjust and conform to the dominant values of the new environment; the conversion efforts of co-workers, shop stewards, party and union militants; gratitude for Communist assistance and attention; and the lack of strong prior party loyalties."[82]

What is striking about this list is that none of the items inherently or automatically work in favor of radicalization or turbulence.   If the word "Communist" were deleted from the quotation, it would be neutral in its implications for political trends. Absence of strong prior loyalties is merely a facilitating factor giving the advantage to whatever influences prevail in those institutions and neighborhoods where migrants cluster.   In Italy, unlike most modernizing nations, urban growth and rapid industrial growth have gone hand in hand.   Therefore, many migrants find factory work.   Moreover, many factories and unions are Communist-dominated.

[23]

The factory is an especially strong source of pressures toward conformity. Southern migrants hide their right-wing political pasts and to ingratiate themselves with their new co-workers, as well as to feel more integrated, they become extreme revolutionaries—in the forefront of most strikes and demonstrations.[83]

In other modernizing countries, far fewer migrants find factory employment. Moreover, in Latin American, Middle Eastern, or Asian cities, Communist-controlled unions or industries are less common than in Italy. Therefore, those migrants who do find factory jobs are less likely to find themselves surrounded by party members. Those who instead become domestic servants, street vendors, or apprentices in artisan shops may be equally eager for acceptance and approval by their new associates, but are hardly likely to turn Communist for this reason. Even in Italy, Fried notes that "many migrants enter work environments with pro-Fascist sympathies, such as domestic service and the various governmental bureaucracies, and vote in accord with their new surroundings."[84]

Gratitude for assistance and attention also has no built-in radical bias. In Italy the Communist party was the first of the major political forces to respond to the problems and opportunities created by the mass influx.

The first conference on immigration problems was held by them in 1957. In October, 1958, Palmiro Togliatti reported to the Central Committee that internal migration, still not yet massive in proportions, was about to alter the geographical, occupational, and political balance of power in the country; he called for study of the factors behind migration and for party efforts to assist and mobilize the migrants. The Communists held two conventions on the problem in 1962 and organized a highly effective campaign to aid the incoming migrants and to become the political party of the migrants à la Tammany Hall. The Communists became the major political force in the immigrant neighborhoods, with a practical monopoly of propaganda, organization, and initiative.[85]

Fried goes on to note that "the effectiveness of the Communist campaign was directly related to the almost complete lack of any attempt by the Italian state to guide the migration process and ease the resulting dislocations." Catholic organizations began to heed the problem in 1960, and within the next few years organized themselves to compete for the loyalties of the migrants.[86] But it is fair to assume that Catholic efforts had not caught up

[24]

with the Communist lead at the time that Fried collected his evidence. As the reference to Tammany Hall makes clear, Communists have no monopoly on gratitude for services rendered. A number of Latin American parties have developed patron-client relations in the slums and squatter settlements in the past few years. The technique is available to any energetic party interested in a mass base.

The final element of Fried's list, the "conversion efforts of co-workers, shop stewards, union and party militants," is simply the mirror image of the migrants' desire to be accepted and their appreciation for assistance and attention.

4. CONCLUSIONS

Two points emerge more clearly as a result of this brief glance at recent Italian experience. First, political socialization appears to be much more important in determining migrants' political behavior than are assumed widespread psychological characteristics of anomie and frustration. The migrants' political behavior is not primarily a reflection of the trauma of migration. Rather, it flows from the political attitudes and patterns of behavior migrants bring with them from the country (or the relative absence of clearly formulated attitudes and fixed behavior patterns) and from an active process of political socialization through situations and agents to which they are exposed in the city.

The second point is a corollary of the first. If migrants' political behavior is best viewed as a result of political socialization under a given set of circumstances (some of which are common to migrants everywhere, and some of which are more or less unique), then there is little reason to assume an inherent or automatic radicalizing bias to the process. To be more accurate, there is some basis for this assumption, but the mechanisms depart rather widely from those suggested by the standard theories on the subject. Urban political socialization may be biased in favor of radical parties, or more generally extremist parties of the right or left, to the extent that such parties tend to be more aggressive and efficient in seeking and mobilizing mass support. Whether and to what degree this condition holds varies from country to country, and changes over time within particular countries. The appropriate focus of inquiry, then, is not the migrants' autonomous perceptions and emotions, but the active politicizing institutions and influences in individual nations or, better, in specific cities, to which they are exposed.

A final point regarding analysis of migrants' political behavior was made earlier, but bears repeating. Migrants into any metropolitan area vary widely in degree of prior urban exposure, education and skills, wealth and contacts, occupation and status, and political background. It is pointless to try to generalize about such a heterogeneous collection. However, migrants do constitute more than a majority of most of the major cities of the developing world. At any given time, a very significant fraction of the urban population has arrived within the previous five years. The question of how different groups of recent migrants are integrated into the political life of the city is important. It can only be pursued by drawing appropriate distinctions among groups of migrants, and examining the predispositions and the influences bearing on each separately.

CHAPTER II

THE RADICAL MARGINALS

Overurbanization . . . is well calculated to provoke the maximum discontent in the population. Faced with idle, impoverished, and rootless urban masses, the government is forced to take drastic action or to allow itself to be displaced by a new revolutionary group. Since economic development is often hindered by outmoded institutional and political arrangements, the role of urbanization in fostering revolutionary activity (whether communist or not) can be said to be potentially favorable to change.[1]

Kingsley Davis and
Hilda Golden

Feelings of relative reward are replaced by feelings of relative deprivation as urban living makes socio-economic inequality more visible. The rewarding comparison with a rural life fades into the past, and gives way to a damaging comparison with higher standards of living. . . . [These observed standards] probably tend to heighten the level of aspiration of many. To the extent that these aspirations are frustrated, they are open to extreme leftist indoctrination. . . . The process of radicalization seems to be dependent upon the race between urbanization, which heightens the level of aspirations for increasing numbers of people, and industrialization, which satisfies them.[2]

Glaucio Soares

1. *The Theory*

To exorcise the myth of the disruptive migrants is to raise a new spectre: that of the radical poor. Each part of the explanation for recent migrants' political passivity has a second aspect. If migrants feel an initial sense of progress as they look back on their former circumstances, what happens when their memories of earlier misery fade? If low levels of political awareness, deference to authority, and perhaps political conservatism are part of the rural baggage migrants carry with them, what happens after prolonged urban exposure? Perhaps the real threat of destabilization inherent in the urban explosion is not the influx of new migrants, but their absorption over time into the simmering

[27]

urban environment. To the extent that migrants establish themselves in the city, shed their sense of strangeness and diffidence, discard their rural outlook, in short, are no longer migrants but urbanites, but fail to find decent jobs or housing, they may be expected to react to economic deprivation with frustration and political aggressiveness. Migration remains in the picture only as the source of a constant flow of new arrivals, depressing wages, swelling the supply of unskilled or semi-skilled labor, matching or outpacing efforts to improve housing and services.

Glaucio Soares states this "radicalization theory" particularly clearly. He argues that urbanization without industrialization creates a growing gap between aspirations and achievement. The resulting frustration is likely to be expressed as political aggression, specifically, radicalism.

The central condition the radicalization theory assumes is widespread economic and social marginality. On this point, it differs from more general theories of the inherently radicalizing characteristics of the city, and explicitly contradicts theories which stress the radicalizing role of the factory. Compare Soares' statement at the opening of this chapter with the following:

> The city is the symbol and the reality of modern industrial civilization. It concentrates people joined by nothing other than the accidents of employment and the necessity of earning a living in industry or service. It is a visible demonstration of the soullessness and alienation of the machine age. . . . Its crowded conditions, the friendless intimacy into which it forces the proletariat, the contrasts, visible to hundreds of thousands, between wealth and poverty, between crime and the protection afforded by authority to the rich and privileged, are in themselves lessons in the class struggle.[3]

Ulam, discussing nineteenth-century urbanization, equates the growth of cities and industrialization. Both, in his view, create in the working class as a whole a sense of disorder, crowding, and oppressive authority. These conditions contrast with an idealized memory of rural life.

> To the city proletarian, who has not yet lost his roots in the country, it is the place where he had status and stable livelihood, where the system of authority, being traditional, appeared less oppressive.[4]

Soares makes no such assumptions about rural life or memories of it. Where Ulam fuses urbanization and industrialization,

[28]

Soares sees two separate though related processes. The roots of radicalism lie precisely in the lag between urban growth and industrial progress. Therefore radicalism may be expected to affect not the entire working class, but that part of it which does not find factory employment, or, by implication, other reasonably steady and well-paid work. Radicalism is a function of marginality.

The "second generation theory" is a modified version of the radicalization theory. For example, Talton Ray, writing about Venezuelan *barrio* youths in their teens and early twenties, notes:

> Several factors work against their adapting to their barrio status. They have grown up, for the most part, in the cities and are not aware of how much less satisfactory life in the countryside can be. Their education is more advanced than their elders'. As barrio residents, they have had far more exposure to the world of party politics than their parents had at the same age. A significant number have already had experience in taking political action, and the parties that have given them this experience usually are not the traditional parties. . . . Their situation will seem worse to them than it was to their parents. As a generation they will be more aware of what they want and what they do not have. Although they should be more qualified for employment, they will still find it very difficult to secure. . . . They will be more alert to their political strength and the means available for voicing their demands.[5]

S. H. Sewell, after stressing the moderate nature of political views and behavior in Turkey's *geçekondu* (squatter settlements), concludes his study as follows:

> The *geçekondu* migrants are relatively close to a common age and have spawned a prodigiously large second generation. This second generation will be reaching maturity in about a decade, and they will not have the close ties to the village, nor will they have the memory of personal improvement between a life in the village and a life in the city. They will compare their life with that of other city dwellers. If the amenities of city life continue to be withheld, the Turkish administrators may discover that, by ignoring the needs of the *geçekondu* population, they have generated just the class hatred they tried to prevent.[6]

S. P. Huntington predicts:

> In Asia and Latin America, as well as in North America, urban violence, political and criminal, is due to rise as the proportion of natives to immigrants in the cities rises. At some point, the slums

of Rio and Lima, of Lagos and Calcutta, like those of Harlem and Watts, are likely to be swept by social violence, as the children of the city demand the rewards of the city.[7]

Daniel Goldrich, analyzing squatter settlements in Lima, Peru, and Santiago, Chile, comes to similar if less chilling conclusions by a slightly different route. Noting that the *pobladores* have accomplished a good deal individually and collectively, but lack recognition and status in the broader community, he concludes:

> If they do not find support, if neither their achievements nor they themselves win respect and recognition somewhere in the society at large, then the following consequences seem likely and only a few years away. Children, raised with much parental ambition and sacrifice, may fail to find the means to get ahead or become embarrassed about living in such settlements. In either event, high intrafamilial tensions and a high level of self-hate among the youth may result. Thus, the next generation could greatly raise the costs to the nation of malintegration of the settlements, either by venting their frustrations in political opposition, across-the-board delinquency, or extreme privatization. Opposition would seem to be promoted to the extent that they are socialized in a home and community environment where the political system is regarded as bad.[8]

To the extent that the radicalization theory is valid, its implications are far-reaching. In virtually all of Latin America, much of Asia, and to some extent in Africa, large and growing parts of the urban population have long experience in the city or are urban-born, but have not found a secure niche in the urban economic and social system. Moreover, the urban marginal population is not likely to be absorbed for many decades, perhaps as much as a half-century in some countries.

The Economic Commission for Latin America has developed a simple model which provides some sense of the dimensions of the problem.[9] ECLA assumes a hypothetical country with a labor force of ten million. Of these, three million are urban, including two million gainfully employed and one million "marginals." In the model, the urban labor force expands at a rate determined jointly by the rates of growth of the national labor force and of employment in agriculture. In turn, the rates of expansion of the urban labor force and the increase in adequately paid urban jobs together determine whether the city's marginal work-

Figure 1

Trends in Urban Marginal Workers at Different Rates of Growth of National Labor Force

(Assuming supply of adequate urban jobs grows at an average of 5 per cent annually)

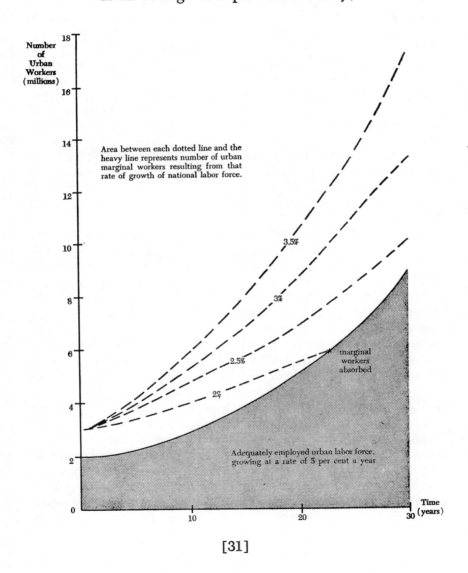

ers are gradually absorbed into the productive labor force or whether they remain a constant or even a growing part of the city's population.

The model can be used to project trends in the marginal urban labor force under various alternative sets of assumptions. For example, let us assume that rural employment is growing slowly—at 1.5 per cent a year[10]—and the number of productive urban jobs is increasing at approximately 5 per cent annually. Under these conditions, the size of the total urban labor force and of the urban marginal group is determined by the rate of growth of the national labor force, as shown in Figure 1. The model demonstrates that (under the assumed conditions) a slow annual rate of growth of 2 per cent in the nation's total labor force will permit the marginal urban working class to be absorbed into the productive urban work force in roughly two decades. However, if the national labor force is growing more rapidly—at 2.5 per cent a year—there will be little reduction in the number of urban marginal workers during the thirty years covered by the model. At still more rapid rates of growth of the national labor force, the number of marginal urban workers increases over the thirty years.

Which rates of growth of the total labor force are most realistic? The answer varies from region to region. The Economic Commission for Asia and the Far East anticipates that India's entire labor force will expand at a rate of less than 2 per cent per year during the quarter century from 1956 to 1981.[11] In Latin America, labor forces are probably growing more rapidly. The Economic Commission for Latin America estimates that the manpower supply between ages fifteen and sixty-five will have increased by 32 per cent during the 1960's in the region as a whole,[12] implying an average annual growth rate of 2.8 per cent. A growing proportion of young men and women probably are postponing their entry into the labor market to complete more years of school. On the other hand, better health care may slightly increase the number of older persons who are able to remain in the labor market up to age sixty-five. Therefore, while the age groups between fifteen and sixty-five are growing at 2.8 per cent, the average annual rate of increase in those actively seeking work may be slightly lower—perhaps 2.5 or 2.6 per cent.

What would happen if adequate urban employment ex-

[32]

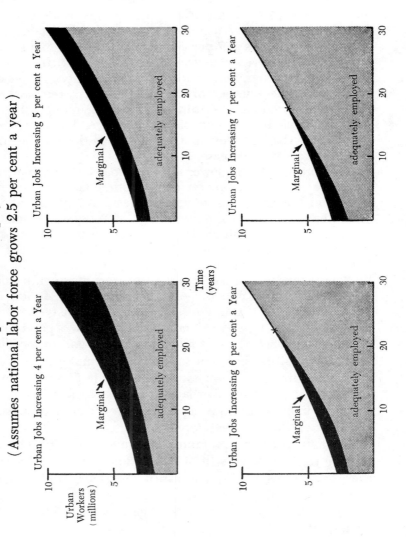

Figure 2

Trends in Urban Marginal Workers at Different Rates of Growth
of Adequate Urban Employment

(Assumes national labor force grows 2.5 per cent a year)

panded more slowly or more rapidly than 5 per cent a year? Figure 2 holds constant the rate of growth of the national labor force (at 2.5 per cent, a not unrealistic rate for Latin America), and lets the rate of growth of adequate urban employment vary between 4 and 7 per cent a year. If the number of good urban jobs increases at 7 per cent a year, the marginal labor force is absorbed in seventeen years. At 6 per cent, the process of absorbing the marginal workers takes twenty-two years. At 5 per cent, the number of marginal workers remains roughly the same throughout the thirty-year period, though it is beginning to shrink by the end of that time. A 4 per cent rate of growth of urban employment implies that the number of marginal workers will increase.

Unfortunately, the lower rates of expansion of urban employment are probably more realistic. Both poor data on employment and the fuzzy distinction between "adequate" and "marginal" employment bar more than the roughest estimate. Industrial employment in modern factories expanded at an average annual rate of 3.3 per cent in Latin America during the 1950's, but even in 1960 it represented only 15 per cent of non-agricultural employment. Other types of reasonably secure and adequately paid urban employment, including basic services (transport, power, etc.) and government service, may have grown somewhat more rapidly, at rates of 4.6 and 3.8 per cent. Employment in construction, trade and finance, and unspecified services grew still faster,[13] but much of this employment may well have been "marginal." An estimate of a 4 to 5 per cent increase per year in remunerative urban employment may not be far from the mark in many Latin American cities—too slow to make much of a dent on the marginal population.

Family planning programs may eventually be effective in slowing the rate of growth of population and labor force. However, even spectacularly successful programs would have little effect on the rate of growth of the labor force during the next thirty years, since that rate is largely determined by children already born. Therefore, unless the rate of growth of urban employment in Latin America accelerates from 4 or 5 per cent a year to 6 or 7 per cent or better, marginal urban populations will continue to be major features of the urban scene for several

[34]

decades. An increasing part of the urban poor will be urban-born.

2. *The Evidence*

In short, the conditions assumed by the radicalization theory are widespread, growing in scale, and likely to be of some duration. Therefore, the theory's predictions of turbulence and extremism are highly relevant and disturbing. But how valid is the theory? Despite its importance, it remains virtually untested. This is in part because severe practical problems hamper efforts at verification or disproof.

As usual, definition difficulties head the list. It is not difficult to define "new migrants" as those with less than an (arbitrary) number of years of residence in the city where they now live.[14] But who are the "urban marginals"? Are they the people who live in slums and squatter settlements? The unskilled and illiterate? Those who, regardless of skill or education, do not hold fairly steady, relatively decently-paid jobs? Those with very low incomes?

These criteria overlap, but far from completely. Many squatter-settlement and slum residents have steady jobs and some education. Some unskilled workers have steady jobs, while some skilled workers, particularly those with artisan skills, may earn a precarious living. Moreover, each of these criteria—housing, education and skill level, occupational status, occupational security, income—is a scale, not a dichotomy. Those at the very bottom of each scale are clearly "marginal," at least with respect to that characteristic. But it is arbitrary to draw a line somewhere on the scale and declare that those below the line are "marginal" while those above it are non-marginal or integrated.

Moreover, we are interested in changes in attitudes and status over decades. During such periods, standards rise: a person with two or three years' education might not have been regarded as marginal on that criterion two decades ago but might well be so classified today. Like Alice, the urban poor may find that they must run to keep their place.

If relatively objective criteria like occupation and education are ambiguous measures of marginality, it goes without saying that more subjective indices like social status, cultural integra-

[35]

tion, or political influence are impractical yard-sticks, even though they are important aspects of the concept of marginality.

Suppose, however, that we agree upon an arbitrary definition of marginality. Soares, for example, took the category "unskilled labor" as a rough equivalent. The radicalization theory states that with increased urban exposure, those classified as marginal will tend to grow more radical. The hypothesis could best be tested by drawing separate samples of new unskilled and skilled migrants in several cities, recording their political attitudes and behavior to establish a baseline, and retesting the same groups periodically over ten or twenty years. Being impatient for results, however, scholars are more likely to draw and compare samples representing different degrees of urban experience: newcomers, migrants with a number of years' residence, and perhaps urban-born. In principle, such samples should be matched for sex, age, education, family status, and other variables likely to affect political attitudes independently of urban experience. For example, if the average age of the sample of newcomers were substantially lower than that of the more established migrants, different political attitudes might reflect differences in age-related social position and familial responsibilities and perhaps different "political generations" rather than differences in length of urban exposure.[15] Such controls are certainly feasible. In practice, however, they have not been applied in those few studies which purport to test the theory of radicalization.

Such studies have also been hampered by the difficulty of devising an adequate index of radicalism. Even where voting data are available and the party system includes a party which is both legal and clearly radical, it may be misleading to equate support for this party in any single election with a sustained radical orientation. Survey questions which probe for radical sentiment are likely to produce evasive replies, hence resort to indices which do not alarm respondents, but also do not measure radicalism very well.

Soares' survey of class identification and political affiliation in Rio de Janeiro, which provides part of the evidence for his theory of radicalization, illustrates these problems. The survey, conducted in 1960, covered a cross-section of all classes and included two hundred sixty-eight skilled and unskilled manual workers.

[36]

Among these workers, Soares found that "radicalism," measured in terms of support for the Brazilian Labor Party (PTB) was highest among unskilled (marginal) laborers who had long urban experience. His data are summarized in Table 2:

Table 2[16]

"Radicalism" Among Manual Workers, Rio, 1960

Skill level	Length of Urban Residence				
	Less than 20 Years		*More than 20 Years*		
	Per Cent For PTB	Sample Size	Per Cent For PTB	Sample Size	
Skilled workers	38	(92)	37	(72)	(164)
Unskilled workers	32	(62)	50	(42)	(104)

The data present at least two problems. First, there is the question of interpreting support for the Brazilian Labor Party as evidence of radical sentiment. An expressed preference for the PTE certainly indicates interest in social reform, but falls well short of implying desire for a radical transformation of the social and economic system. Second, Soares did not test his findings against controls for differences in education, age, or other variable which might be masked by skill level, and which might be partl or largely responsible for his results.

Soares' data can be roughly replicated using data from Almond and Verba's surveys in Mexico. For their study of the "civic culture" in Mexico, a sample of somewhat over a thousan was drawn from all levels of urban society. (Interviews wer conducted only in cities of 10,000 or more).[17] Four hundre and fifty-six respondents were skilled or unskilled manual worl ers, domestic servants, or the wives of such workers. Amon this working class group, two hundred and thirty-five can l clearly identified either as rural-to-urban migrants (born in vi lages of less than 5,000 and residing in cities of 50,000 or more or as big-city residents born and bred.

Party preferences cannot be used to test "radicalism" with this group, since none of the two hundred and thirty-five su ported the leftist Partido Popular. However, two questions techniques of exercising influence give us some clues on th willingness to exert strong pressure or resort to violence. The fi

[37]

question lists five techniques of influencing the government, including working through personal connections, writing to government officials, forming a group, working through an established party, or demonstrating. Eleven per cent of the sub-sample of two hundred and thirty-five chose demonstrations from this list. Respondents were also asked to name the most effective way to influence the government, without referring to any list. Five per cent suggested violence. If the two hundred and thirty-five are sub-divided by length of urban residence and skill level, there is a rough pattern of greater militance among skilled workers with longer urban experience, but no such pattern appears among the unskilled. However, the numbers are too small to be statistically significant.

Table 3a.

Mexican Working Class People Selecting Demonstrations or Violence as the Most Effective Ways to Influence Government

Item and skill level	Length of Urban Experience			
	Less than 20 Years		*More than 20 Years*	
	Per Cent	Sample Size	Per Cent	Sample Size
Choose demonstrations:				
Skilled	8	(50)	13	(107)
Unskilled	15	(41)	4	(28)
Choose Violence:				
Skilled	4	(51)	7	(110)
Unskilled	2	(42)	4	(27)

Soares' Rio sample was entirely male. The women included in the Mexican sub-sample were disproportionately concentrated among the unskilled. To check whether this factor was responsible for the non-militance of the unskilled in the Mexican sample, the data was recomputed for men separately. The same pattern emerges still more sharply. Higher militance among skilled workers with long urban experience may reflect greater union exposure. Whatever the reasons for the patterns, however, they run directly counter to Soares' theory and to his Rio findings.

Daniel Goldrich, studying partisan affiliations in a squatter settlement and a public housing project in Santiago, Chile, found that FRAP, the Marxist coalition of Socialists and Communists,

Table 3b

*Mexican Male Workers Selecting Demonstrations or
Violence as the Most Effective Ways to
Influence Government*

Item and skill level	Length of Urban Experience			
	Less than 20 Years		More than 20 Years	
	Per Cent	Sample Size	Per Cent	Sample Size
Choose demonstrations:				
Skilled	5	(20)	14	(57)
Unskilled	15	(13)	0	(7)
Choose Violence:				
Skilled	0	(19)	10	(58)
Unskilled	0	(13)	0	(7)

appeared to be recruiting disproportionately from among younger voters, and from newer migrants. FRAP supporters also tended to come from more highly educated families and were more likely than non-partisans or Christian Democratic Party supporters to hold skilled or semi-skilled jobs.[18] Goldrich does not present data relating FRAP support simultaneously to length of urban experience and skill level. But his findings for the two variables taken separately do not jibe with Soares' data from his Rio sample.

Data from the study by Alex Inkeles and his associates of the impact of factory experience on workers' attitudes lends somewhat greater support to the radicalization theory. For this study, surveys were conducted among large samples of factory workers and smaller control groups of urban non-industrial workers and of cultivators in six developing nations. The Inkeles surveys did not inquire into party preferences. However, in Chile and Argentina (though not in the other four countries) respondents were asked what kind of social and economic change was desirable in their country — rapid and drastic change, moderate change, no change, or a return to earlier ways. A three-point scale was constructed from replies on two such questions. Table 4 shows the pattern which emerges if respondents are grouped by skill and occupation, and by degree of urban experience, and mean scores on the radicalism scale are compared across these groups. Examining only the three migrant categories, unskilled and semi-skilled migrant factory workers seem

[39]

TABLE 4

Radicalism and Urban Experience in Chile and Argentina

(Mean scores on "radicalism scale": high figure indicates more "radical":
possible range 1-3)

Country and skill/occupation	Sample Size	Years Urban Since Age 15				
Argentina		0-4	5-11	12 or more	Urban-born	Average
Unskilled factory workers	58	1.17	1.75	1.75	2.09	1.88
Semi-skilled factory workers	421	1.35	1.65	1.92	1.98	1.84*
Skilled factory workers	110	c	1.86	1.56	2.13	2.07
Low-level non-factory workers	24	—	c	c	2.40	2.33
Higher-level non-factory workers	23	c	—	c	2.35	2.39
Chile		0-2	3-10	11 or more	Urban-born	Average
Unskilled factory workers	163	2.00	1.91	2.26	2.20	2.10
Semi-skilled factory workers	228	1.79	1.82	2.11	2.13	2.03
Skilled factory workers	292	2.33	2.02	1.98	2.36	2.22*
Low-level non-factory workers	58	c	2.08	2.17	2.26	2.22
Higher-level non-factory workers	45	—	1.80	2.00	2.56	2.42

*Chi-square value significant at or above the .002 level.

a/Low-level non-industrial workers in the Argentine sample include newsvenders, peddlers, porters, kiosk operators, waiters. In the Chile sample, they include peddlers, vendors in open markets, delivery boys, loaders, stevedores, floor waxers, errand boys.

b/Higher-level non-industrial workers in the Argentine sample include artisans, barbers, cab drivers, salesmen. In the Chile sample, they include owners of small self-run businesses, taxi or bus drivers, and small artisans (plumber, shoemaker, electrician).

c/Mean scores based on 1 or 2 respondents have been omitted from the table.

to become more "radical" with longer urban experience, while skilled workers become less disposed to radical change as they gain urban experience. The most clearly marginal group — low level non-industrial workers — also seems to become more radical in Chile, although the trend is hard to verify because the sub-sample includes so few newcomers to the city. (In Argentina the sub-sample of non-industrial workers is almost entirely urban-born.) The urban-born in all sub-groups are consistently more favorable to rapid change than any of the migrants. However, in all but two sub-groups the relationship between urban experience and radicalism is too weak to be statistically significant. Moreover, while the questions comprising the scale mea-

[40]

sure receptivity to rapid social change and the recognition of need for such change, they leave open the political means of bringing about such change. They are not clear indicators of political radicalism.

Studies of class voting patterns and analyses of the social origins of those who take part in urban violence do not distinguish among degrees of urban experience nor between established and marginal workers. Therefore they do not really test the hypothesis. But since good tests are not available, such studies at least give us some data on the political behavior of the urban population in general.

In India, survey data collected before the 1966 elections in four major metropolitan cities (Bombay, Calcutta, Delhi, and Madras) found that those in the lowest income group (earning less than Rs. 150 monthly) were no more and no less likely to support extremist parties of the right or left than were more affluent groups. Three to 4 per cent said that they planned to vote for Communist candidates for the Lok Sabha and the state legislature, 4 per cent supported the Jan Sangh, and 2 per cent favored the Swatantra Party.[19] An earlier, all-urban poll in 1965 found 4 per cent of those earning under Rs. 75 a month and 2 per cent of those earning between Rs. 75 and Rs. 150 supporting the left Communists, compared to only 1 per cent of the total sample — still hardly persuasive evidence of extensive radicalization.[20]

An analysis of recent presidential elections in Caracas, Venezuela, and in Santiago, Chile, finds that support for left-wing candidates is indeed higher in low income districts. (See Tables 5a and 5b.) However, only in Santiago, where the Socialist and Communist parties are long-established, well-organized, and have campaigned actively in recent years in low income urban neighborhoods, do large numbers of low income voters support the radical parties. The Socialist and Communist parties in Chile are traditionally the parties of organized urban labor, and it is fair to assume that much of their support in the working class districts of Greater Santiago comes from semi-skilled and skilled workers regularly employed in industry and modern services, as distinct from the marginal workers at the center of the radicalization theory.

This is not to argue that support for FRAP is not also high

Table 5a[21]

Socio-economic Level and Left-wing Voting in Metropolitan Caracas

Parish*	Per cent supporting PCV 1958	Per cent supporting Villalba** 1963
Low income parishes		
Sucre	7.7	14.0
Antimano	4.7	11.1
La Vega	5.5	12.4
La Pastora	8.5	11.2
Catedral	9.0	13.1
San Juan	7.0	12.2
*"Silk Stocking" district***	3.1	5.1
City total	6.7	10.8

* Classified according to rough correlation between socio-economic level and the city's geographic structure; low income parishes clustering at the west end and wealthy areas at the east.

** The Communist Party of Venezuela was barred from participation in the 1963 elections because of its terrorist activities. Jóvito Villalba, nominee of the basically middle class Union Republicana Democratica, offered the furthest left alternative in the sense of calling for rapid and extensive social reform, and also promised to lift the suspension of the PCV and its MIR ally.

*** Includes El Rosal, La Castellana, Los Palos Grandes, Country Club, Altamira, La Floresta, Campo Alegre, and Bello Campo precincts of Chacao Municipality and Las Mercedes and Chuao precincts of Baruta Municipality.

among marginals. Barrancas is the poorest commune among those of Greater Santiago. As of 1960, only 35 per cent of its population were engaged in manufacturing and construction, in contrast to from 45 to 52 per cent in the other working class communes. However, in both elections support for FRAP in Barrancas was comparable with that in other low-rent districts. Urban marginal workers may indeed be mobilized for radical causes. But there is little evidence that they are especially available to left-wing groups, and some reason to believe that particularly vigorous organizational efforts are required to arouse their interest and capture their loyalty.

Turning from elections to violence, several studies suggest that the poorest urban groups are not likely to be disproportion-

Socio-economic Level and Left-wing Voting in Greater Santiago

Commune*	Per cent supporting Allende (FRAP)		Commune vote as per cent	
	1958	1964	1958	1964
Low-rent communes				
Barrancas	37.3	48.1	1.9	3.0
La Granja	35.6	48.9	1.4	3.0
Renca	38.4	43.4	2.0	2.5
Conchali	36.8	41.1	4.4	6.4
High-rent communes				
Las Condes	18.3	21.7	2.9	4.2
Providencia	12.3	16.9	5.8	4.9
City total	27.8	34.9	(100.0)	(100.0)

* Low-rent communes include those in which over 80 per cent of the population live in accommodations classified as "low-rent" in the 1952 census. High-rent communes include those where more than half the population live in high-rent residences. Five communes, including the very heavily populated commune of Santiago proper, fall between these extremes and are omitted from the table.

ately involved in urban political disturbances. Myron Weiner, surveying demonstrations and violent incidents in Calcutta during the 1950's, concludes:

> Demonstrators, then, come from many social classes, but the demonstrations most likely to be violent are those in which the middle classes form the core. . . . Working class strikes in Calcutta only rarely involve violence and almost never involve the entire city. . . . In contrast, middle class agitations in Calcutta have involved the most violence: the strike against an increase in train fares, the strike for an increase in teachers' salaries, and a small but violent agitation in 1954 of orthodox Hindus for a government ban on the slaughter of cows. It was the threatened Post and Telegraph workers' strike, the Bank Employee strike, and the Bengal-Bihar merger agitation which immediately alerted the police for possible large scale violence.[23]

Historical evidence confirms the impression that those on the margins of the city's economic and social structure do not play a major role in radical movements or political turbulence. Tilly writes of nineteenth-century Paris:

The great Parisian series of strikes in 1840 brought out the tailors, papermakers, nailmakers, carters, wainwrights, masons, stonecutters, locksmiths, turners, carpenters, shoemakers, spinners, bookbinders and bakers — mostly men from the skilled, established crafts. . . . The "despair" and "exasperation" . . . were real enough. The point is that they were articulated and acted upon by segments of the Parisian working class already politically alert, organized, integrated into the life of the city. Not, that is, the uprooted, outcast, dangerous classes. The studies that have been done of participants in diverse outbreaks in Paris between 1830 and 1860 point in the same direction. For the Revolution of 1830, Adeline Daumard observes that "artisans on the border between the common people and the bourgeoisie were at the core of the insurgents," and David Pinkney's careful enumerations agree.[24]

3. *Where the Theory Goes Wrong*

The radicalization theory, in contrast to the myth of the disruptive migrants, is probably overstated rather than wrong. The cities unquestionably heighten aspirations. There is no blinking the fact that living conditions are abysmal. The contrast between desires and reality must surely generate discontent. To the extent that the poor are exposed to political appeals through the mass media and campaigns, are placed in contact with officials and politicians, or associate with more politically sophisticated neighbors or co-workers, their political consciousness must increase. Sooner or later, frustration based on felt deprivation must find at least partial expression in political action.

The problem lies not with the broad outlines of the theory, but with its failure to consider rates and leakages. If expectations rise more slowly than aspirations, and if small improvements are felt as real progress, or if the society is viewed as essentially open despite individual disappointments, then frustration may grow more slowly than the theorists assume. If political awareness spreads gradually, discontinuously, and unevenly among the urban poor; if the connection between political awareness and political action is less automatic and more influenced by the political and social setting than the theory implies; and if the urban poor are less disposed to blame the government for their troubles than are the more privileged, then the likelihood that frustration will be channeled into political protest is

[44]

reduced regardless of the level of frustration. A great deal of discontent will "leak" out of the political system described by the model into other, apolitical responses. Finally, the probability that political protest will take the specific forms of violence and/or radicalism is strongly conditioned by the existing political climate and institutions. Survey data and studies of mobility and politicization provide some clues on these points.

The aspiration-achievement gap: aspirations. In view of the fact that the concept of the aspirations-achievement gap is widely used, it is somewhat surprising that the relationship between urban exposure and aspirations has not yet been systematically examined. However, the Inkeles surveys provide some clues on the question.

Housing is a major component of material well-being. In Chile and Argentina, urban workers were shown photographs of several different grades of housing. They were asked both to identify the picture most like their current house, and to indicate the kind of house they would like "in order to feel really satisfied and comfortable." By numbering each grade of housing, from poorest to best, the "housing aspiration gap" between an individual's desired and current housing can be calculated. Looking at all migrants as a group, the housing aspiration gap narrows steadily with longer urban residence.

Table 6

Urban Experience and Housing Satisfaction

Country	Index	Years Urban Since Age 15		
Argentina		0-4	5-11	12 or more
	Mean score on "gap" scale (Possible range 1-7: high score indicates dissatisfaction)	3.17	2.72	2.25
	Per cent satisfied with current housing (no gap)	14	34	43
Chile		0-2	3-10	11 or more
	Mean score on "gap" scale (Possible range 1-6: high score indicates dissatisfaction)	2.92	2.73	2.35
	Per cent satisfied with current housing (no gap)	22	27	37

[45]

However, if migrants are sub-divided by skill level, it becomes clear that while skilled and semi-skilled workers are better housed the longer they are in the city, unskilled workers make little progress. In fact, in Chile the proportion of unskilled workers housed in slum or semi-slum dwellings is larger among the long-established than among the newcomers. Correspond-

Table 7

Skill Level, Urban Experience, and Housing Satisfaction

(Mean Score on Housing Aspiration Gap Scale:
High Score Indicates Dissatisfaction.)

Country and skill/occupation*	Sample Size	Years Urban Since Age 15		
Argentina (scale range 1-7)		0-4	5-11.	12 or more
Unskilled factory worker	(53)	3.50	3.08	3.75
Semi-skilled factory worker	(335)	3.14	2.64	2.21
Skilled factory worker	(84)	—	3.00	1.86
Chile (scale range 1-6)		0-2	3-10	11 or more
Unskilled factory worker	(138)	2.80	2.70	3.00
Semi-skilled factory worker	(211)	3.07	2.73	2.08
Skilled factory worker	(259)	2.86	2.80	2.27
Low-level non-factory worker	(52)	—	2.64	2.50
Higher-level non-factory worker	(34)	—	2.67	2.00

*In Argentina, almost all non-factory workers sampled are urban-born, and these occupation categories are therefore omitted in this and later tables.

ingly, while the level of housing *desired* by the unskilled workers shows no clear upward trend, the unfilled "gap" is larger for the longer established unskilled migrants than for those who are newcomers to the city. The widening, however, is hardly dramatic; it suggests a persistent desire for decent housing, rather than escalating claims. Another way to assess trends in housing aspirations is to look at the proportions of workers choosing the two highest levels of housing shown (a modern apartment and an upper-middle class house). There is no consistent pattern of increase (or decrease) in the per cent aspiring to "luxury" housing as urban experience increases.

The Inkeles surveys also inquired into job satisfaction among factory workers. In Argentina, Chile, India, and Pakistan,[25] job satisfaction among migrants declines with urban exposure. In Argentina and Chile, as urban experience increases, workers in

Table 8

Skill Level, Urban Experience, and Job Satisfaction
(Mean Score on Job Satisfaction: High Score Indicates Satisfaction.
Possible Range 1-4)

Country and skill/occupation	Sample Size	Years Urban Since Age 15		
Argentina		0-4	5-11	12 or more
Unskilled factory worker	(58)	3.67	2.81	2.75
Semi-skilled factory worker	(417)	3.42	3.23	3.38
Skilled factory worker	(109)	4.00	3.33	3.11
Chile		0-2	3-10	11 or more
Unskilled factory worker	(163)	3.00	2.80	2.68
Semi-skilled factory worker	(228)	2.64	2.91	2.89
Skilled factory worker	(292)	3.44	3.07	3.04
Low-level non-factory worker	(55)	4.00	2.46	3.00
High-level non-factory worker	(45)	—	3.60	3.00
India		0-2	3-8	9 or more
Unskilled factory worker	(383)	2.78	2.86	3.10
Semi-skilled factory worker	(126)	3.01	2.71	2.57
Skilled factory worker	(184)	3.14	2.92	2.69
Low-level non-factory worker	(162)	1.96	2.39	2.32
High-level non-factory worker	(82)	2.11	2.10	2.29
Pakistan		0-2	3-8	9 or more
Unskilled factory worker	(82)	2.67	2.25	2.80
Semi-skilled factory worker	(469)	2.69	2.48	2.56
Skilled factory worker	(53)	3.45	3.20	2.07

all categories except the semi-skilled become less content with their jobs, in roughly the same degree. In India and Pakistan, mean scores for skilled workers drop with urban exposure, but the proportion of satisfied unskilled workers grows. In the Indian sample, the shift is so marked that among migrants with nine or more years of urban residence, more unskilled than skilled workers express satisfaction with their work. Non-factory workers in India also seem to grow more satisfied as they stay longer in the city. Unfortunately, data on job satisfaction among Pakistani urban non-industrial workers are not available.

A great many elements enter into job satisfaction. However, men who are intensely dissatisfied with their wages are not likely to say that they are satisfied or very satisfied with their jobs. Unskilled workers with longer urban experience may be earning, on the average, somewhat more than unskilled newcomers. But it is hard to reconcile a rapid multiplication of material desires with the pattern of job satisfaction among the unskilled in the South Asian samples, or even with the trend toward lower satisfaction which unskilled workers share with other manual workers in the Latin American samples.

The Inkeles surveys also provide some insights regarding aspirations of a non-material kind. Respondents were shown a

Table 9

Skill Level, Urban Experience, and Status Satisfaction

(Mean score on Status Satisfaction: High Score Indicates Satisfaction: Possible Range 1-4)

Country and skill/occupation	Sample Size	Years Urban Since Age 15		
Argentina		0-4	5-11	12 or more
Unskilled factory worker	(58)	2.67	2.44	3.00
Semi-skilled factory worker	(422)	2.88	2.72	2.81
Skilled factory worker	(111)	4.00	2.29	2.22
Chile		0-2	3-10	11 or more
Unskilled factory worker	(164)	2.53	2.57	2.58
Semi-skilled factory worker	(227)	2.93	2.59	2.50
Skilled factory worker	(292)	3.22	2.31	2.52
Low-level non-factory worker	(58)	3.00	2.46	2.17
Higher-level non-factory worker	(45)	—	2.60	2.50

picture of a ladder (or hill) which they were told represented "the social positions of all the people in the country." They were asked where people like themselves stood on the ladder. In Argentina and Chile, they were also asked how satisfied they were with their self-assessed social status. In both countries, the level of status satisfaction drops steadily with longer urban experience among skilled factory workers, and among non-factory workers in Chile. Unskilled workers, in contrast, show roughly constant or even slightly rising degrees of satisfaction with their social standing.

Finally, educational aspirations for one's children climb steadily with urban exposure, not only for migrants as a group, but also for sub-categories classified by skill and education jointly. In Chile and Argentina, respondents were asked not only how many years of education they hoped their sons would receive, but also how much schooling they actually expected

[48]

Table 10

Urban Experience and Aspirations for Son's Education

Country and Index	Years Urban Since Age 15		
Argentina*	0-4	5-11	12 or more
Mean level of schooling desired for son	4.23	4.88	5.02
Mean level of schooling expected for son	3.43	3.49	3.44
Gap	2.17	2.64	2.80
Chile **	0-2	3-10	11 or more
Mean number of years of school desired for son	11.14	12.10	13.19
Mean number of years of school expected for son	6.05	7.14	7.68
Gap	4.09	4.96	5.51

*In the Argentine survey, the amount of education respondents desired for their sons was coded in terms of levels rather than years. Level 1 corresponded to 1 to 3 years' schooling; level 2 comprised 4 to 6 years' education, and so forth through level 7, corresponding to 18 to 20 years' schooling. The difference between level desired and level expected was computed for each respondent, and the "gap" for each group of migrants represents the mean of the "gap scores" for all *individuals* in that group.

**The Chile survey recorded the actual number of years of education respondents desired and expected for their sons. For each group of migrants (recent, less recent, long-established), the mean number of years of school desired and expected was calculated. The "gap" is the difference in these *group* means.

them to attain. The resulting "son's education aspiration gap" widens steadily with urban residence.

If parents' ambitions for their children are likely to be disappointed, are the children themselves more frustrated than their generally patient elders? The Inkeles data give some support to speculation that the second generation is less accepting of material and status deprivation. The samples drawn in Argentina and Chile (though not those in India and Pakistan) include sizeable numbers of urban-born. The urban-born groups in both countries are on the average slightly younger, better educated, and better paid than the migrants, although they are not disproportionately represented among the skilled workers. Their mean scores for job and status satisfaction are generally lower than the migrants' scores. This overall pattern holds in Chile among all skill/occupation groups except, surprisingly, the low-

[49]

Table 11

Aspirations and Satisfaction Among Urban-born Workers Compared with Migrant Workers

Country and Skill Level	Mean Scores: Job Satisfaction (range 1-4)		Mean Scores: Status Satisfaction (range 1-4)		Mean Scores: Housing Gap (range 1-7, 6)		Mean Scores: Current Housing (range 1-7, 6)		Mean Scores: Education Gap	
	migrants	urban-born	migrants	urban-born	migrants	urban-born	migrants	urban-born	migrants	urban-born
Argentina									(measured in levels)	
Unskilled	2.99	3.13	2.72	2.69	3.28	2.10	2.32	2.53	2.62	2.53
Semi-skilled	3.30	3.15	2.58	2.75	2.59	2.29	3.07	3.55	n.a.	
Skilled	3.25	3.32	2.77	2.64	2.22	1.90	3.42	4.08		
Total sample	3.26	3.18	2.36	2.67	2.66	2.19				
Chile									(measured in years)	
Unskilled	2.85	2.67	2.59	2.45	2.82	2.60	2.41	2.38	5.03	5.10
Semi-skilled	2.87	2.72	2.61	2.46	2.59	3.16	2.45	2.02	n.a.	
Skilled	3.08	2.91	2.47	2.27	2.57	2.90	2.64	2.28		
Low non-factory	2.70	2.91	2.85	2.37	2.62	2.83	2.15	2.08		
High non-factory	3.33	3.00	2.56	2.44	2.37	2.61	3.44	2.94		
Total sample	2.94	2.82	2.53	2.38	2.63	2.88				

level non-factory workers, among whom urban-born are on the average more satisfied with their work than migrants doing similar jobs. In Argentina, skilled and unskilled urban-born are more satisfied with both job and status than their migrant counterparts. However, Argentine semi-skilled urban-born are less satisfied, and they dominate the overall results because of their large share in the total sample. As for housing, in Chile the urban-born are consistently less satisfied than migrants, in all skill categories except unskilled factory workers. In Argentina all the urban-born groups are more content with their housing than their migrant counterparts. There is a simple explanation for the contrast: in Chile, migrants are consistently better housed than urban-born, while in Argentina the reverse is true, judging by the respondents' own descriptions of the type of housing they occupied. Finally, as one would expect, the urban-born, themselves better educated than the migrants, want and expect their sons to receive more schooling. The gap between desired and expected levels of sons' education is narrower for urban-born Argentines than for their migrant counterparts. Chilean urbanites anticipate roughly the same discrepancy as do the Chilean migrants between the amount of education they would like to see their sons attain and the amount they expect their sons to actually receive. Table 11 summarizes these comparisons.

These findings are far from conclusive. They suggest, however, that while blue collar aspirations rise with urban exposure, they do not rise particularly rapidly. Moreover, the pattern of expanding desires and increasing sensitivity to social status is clearer among skilled than unskilled. Unfortunately, Inkeles' data on low-level non-industrial workers — the sample most closely approximating the marginal population — is fragmentary and inconsistent. The second generation is indeed less satisfied with manual work and low status than are migrants. However, as will be discussed shortly, occupational mobility among the urban-born is also likely to be greater, leaving open the possibility that higher aspirations are in part matched by higher levels of achievement.

While direct data on the effect of urban experience on aspirations is scarce, there are better documented studies of the urban poor which support the assumption that aspirations rise slowly, particularly among the poorest and least skilled.

[51]

First, those at the very lowest levels are preoccupied with survival.

> Among the urban peasants of the Lower Lower Class in Quere-
> taro a man's complete time and thought seemed to be devoted
> to keeping alive, and pure physical exhaustion numbed any
> stirrings of great ambitions.[26]

Some of those who can think a bit beyond tonight's meal may nonetheless be paralyzed by apathy and hopelessness. Oscar Lewis argues that the culture of poverty

> represents an effort to cope with feelings of hopelessness and
> despair that arise from the realization by the members of the
> marginal communities in these societies of the improbability of
> their achieving success in terms of the prevailing values and
> goals.[27]

Objective barriers to progress come to be reflected in psychological orientations: apathy and conviction of inability to act successfully, hence failure to develop skills, low expectations, and little or no striving.

Many others, while far from paralyzed, may gear their goals of self-improvement to a realistic assessment of their situations. Research on lower and middle class aspirations in the United States (where the poor have long been exposed to higher living standards) shows that the less privileged set modest occupational targets for themselves. These targets may require as much effort as higher goals demand of middle class aspirants: equal ambition may result in quite different goals.[28]

> The first step upward on the ladder of social mobility is always
> one of the most difficult. In Queretaro it consisted first of leav-
> ing work in the fields and finding a job in the city; then of
> moving to another part of Tepetate [the poorest neighborhood
> of the city] or perhaps a *vecindad* nearer the center of town,
> where light and water and perhaps paved streets made life at
> least a trifle more "citified." The older men almost never
> changed, but their sons had ambitions to work with machines or
> at least to acquire some skills with tools. The distinctive thing
> we found was that their ambitions were strictly limited. They
> had little to do with formal education, but boys expressed their
> hopes of becoming masons, shoemakers, or construction workers.
> To achieve these ends, they worked as helpers, and some of the
> young men attended the vocational school at night before it
> closed. Many were successful in their aspirations and became

semi-skilled members of the Upper Lower Class. Only in exceptional cases did they move any higher in the society, for they were always limited by their lack of education, their limited perspectives, and the hungry families which limited their freedom.[29]

Realism may not only trim targets but may also shape values. Miller and Reisman find striving for security and stability to be a central element in the basic values and behavior of regularly employed manual workers in the United States. " 'Getting by' rather than 'getting ahead' . . . is likely to be dominant." Those who aspire to middle class status are viewed as deviants.[30] Herbert Gans describes working class Italians in Boston's West End in similar terms. He stresses the high value placed on sociability, generosity, a helping hand for relatives and neighbors, the comparatively light emphasis on career progress or material accumulation beyond accepted standards of comfort and security, and the explicit rejection of middle class values and patterns.[31] It seems likely that analogous values and perceptions of reality limit expectations among the urban poor in developing nations, especially among migrants who have settled in clusters grouped by village or province of origin.

The aspiration-achievement gap: achievement. Actual accomplishments and the value the poor themselves place on these accomplishments are also crucial in determining the size of the aspiration-achievement gap and the resultant degree of frustration. A sense of progress or achievement may reflect many causes — a better job, higher income, better housing, the grant of title to land and housing previously held on a squatter basis, improved community services, personal recognition and prestige within the immediate community, enhanced group or class prestige within the larger metropolitan or national community, greater personal or communal political power and influence. Most efforts to measure mobility, however, have focussed on individual occupational mobility between generations. Only a handful of studies permit estimates of mobility out of the lowest urban occupational levels in developing countries.

The radicalization theory tacitly assumes substantial immobility at the lowest levels of urban society. This can be tested with data on occupational mobility between generations. Among men whose fathers were unskilled or semi-skilled manual work

[53]

Table 12[32]

Occupational Mobility of Men Whose Fathers Were Unskilled

Occupation level of sons	São Paulo, Brazil (1960) *	Buenos Aires, Argentina (1960) *	Poona, India (1954) *
	Per Cent	Per Cent	Per Cent
1. Unskilled manual domestics, vendors	31.2	21.1	43.2
2. Semi-skilled and skilled manual workers, including supervisory manual grades.	42.0	52.6	26.1
3. Lower-level non-manual, including supervisors, shop and office clerks, small businessmen (1-5 employees).	12.1	21.1	22.2
4. Higher-level non-manual and owners of medium-small businesses.	8.6	2.3	3.2
5. Administrative and executive posts; owners of medium-large stores and factories; liberal professions.	3.0	2.9	1.0
6. High professional and administrative posts.	3.0	0.0	0.8

* The São Paulo sample includes 1,056 men, of whom 338 are sons of un-skilled fathers. The Buenos Aires sample includes 2,078 heads of house-holds, of whom 341 are children of unskilled fathers. The Poona sample includes 4,505 heads of households, of whom 2,004 are sons of unskilled fathers. The percentages in Table 12 are based on the subsamples (chil-dren of unskilled fathers) for each city.

ers, what proportion are themselves at these lowest steps on the occupational ladder? Table 12 shows the occupational levels reached by men whose fathers were unskilled, in sizeable samples drawn in São Paulo, Brazil; Buenos Aires, Argentina; and Poona, India.

Table 12 was constructed by crudely matching the occupational categories used in the three surveys. These categories differed substantially in composition, reflecting divergent research objectives, differences in occupational composition of the labor force, and variation in the social status attached to particular occupations in the three countries. Therefore the table supports only very gross conclusions. Nonetheless, it is clear that in all three cities a majority of those born into the bottom strata rose out of them. Most became skilled manual workers, but substantial fractions found their way into lower- or higher-level non-manual jobs, and a few broad-jumped into higher administrative, business, or professional positions.

Less detailed data for additional cities confirm the impression of considerable movement out of the lowest strata. A probability sample of 1,821 adult men in six major Brazilian cities found 42 per cent of the respondents' fathers had been unskilled, but only a quarter of the respondents themselves were in this bottom category.[33] From this we cannot calculate mobility out of the unskilled group for these six cities, since among the unskilled respondents are some born into that status and some whose fathers stood higher on the ladder. (The more detailed São Paulo data show that 22 per cent of the unskilled manual workers in the current generation had fathers who were more highly skilled.) However, the gross shift in composition itself represents a 40 per cent rate of upward mobility, and net movement out of the unskilled category is probably well over 50 per cent.

All of these studies may understate the extent of upward mobility for urban lower-class groups. Broad occupational categories conceal a substantial range within each category in job prestige, security, pay, and working conditions. Many men who, like their fathers, hold unskilled jobs may nevertheless have made some progress in their own and others' judgment. This is particularly true of the men whose fathers were cultivators. In terms of working conditions, hours, pay, and prestige, most unskilled city jobs are preferred to work in the fields. Moreover, the surveys have a built-in downward bias. Sons' current jobs were compared with their fathers' most recent occupations.

Many of the younger men will rise higher later in their lives. While some fathers may have lost status toward the end of their careers, this is not likely to overbalance the bias caused by the sons' age distribution.

One further point should be considered regarding occupational mobility. Low-status urban children are likely to get more and better education, and have wider contacts and opportunities for apprenticeships and technical training, than their rural counterparts.[34] Therefore, urban-born workers are somewhat more likely to move up from the bottom of the hierarchy. In the Buenos Aires mobility study, 83 per cent of the Buenos Aires-born sons of unskilled fathers had escaped from this lowest occupational category, while 77 per cent of the interior-born sons of unskilled fathers had done so. More important, 35 per cent of the urban-born, compared to only 20 per cent of the migrants, had made the jump to non-manual occupations.[35] Higher occupational mobility may partially offset higher aspirations among the urban-born.

The much-deplored squatter settlements may provide many urban poor with an additional channel of achievement. Such settlements are not usually the first stop for the in-coming migrant, but are more often established by families with longer urban experience. Squatting offers immediate relief from the burden of rent and the threat of eviction, and a long-run prospect of a modicum of comfort and respectability. Where squatters are not harassed by the police, and where terrain and initial density of settlement permit, many shanty-towns evolve over ten or fifteen years into acceptable working class neighborhoods.[36] For example, Goldrich notes that the squatter settlement of Pampa Seca, comprising some 30,000 people on the outskirts of Lima, was begun in 1958. By 1965, "the original shacks of reed matting had been largely replaced by permanent structures in various stages of improvement and elaboration." The community had well-defined, relatively wide unpaved streets. The government had agreed to install water facilities and had laid some piping, although water was not yet available on a piped-in basis.[37] At El Carmen, on the outskirts of Bogotá, residents have been granted permanent title, and three-fourths of the houses are one- or two-story red brick structures with tin roofs. Forty-six per cent of the residents own their homes.[38] As noted earlier, in many cities in Latin America, North Africa, and Turkey, 10 to 40 per cent of the population live in squatter settlements. Not all of these settlements are "self-improving." But for many among the urban poor, squatting is a means of substantial progress.

These fragmentary observations on progress within and movement out of the lowest economic strata do not suggest a rosy picture. They do, however, indicate that modest occupational mobility and probably other types of progress are fairly widely distributed. The picture may be not unlike that which Stephan Thernstrom paints of Newburyport's laborers in the second half of the nineteenth century:

> . . . a large majority of the unskilled laborers in Newburyport and a large majority of their sons remained in the working class throughout the 1850-1880 period. Not one rose from rags to genuine riches. . . . Most of the social gains registered by laborers and their sons during these years were decidedly modest—a move one notch up the occupational scale, the acquisition of a small amount of property. Yet *in their eyes* these accomplishments must have loomed large. . . . The "dream of success" certainly affected these laboring families, but the personal measure of success was modest. By this measure, the great majority of them had indeed "gotten ahead."[39]

Psychologically, such progress may be very important.

> There are indications that upward (or downward) short-distance mobility may be perceived and experienced as deeply important by the mobile subjects, especially in the case of intra-generational mobility. One's ability to discriminate on the basis of prestige is higher when comparing occupations in the proximity of one's own than it is when the occupations are more distant. More important, individual aspiration levels may usually be restricted to a very small range of the social hierarchy.[40]

The Extent of Frustration. The incidence of small advances may help to explain an otherwise puzzling finding in a number of surveys: reports of wide-spread economic stagnation or deterioration, coupled with overwhelming belief that the larger economic and social system is open to talent and hard work. Surveys among lower-class urban people in several countries have asked, "In the past five years, has your economic situation improved, remained the same, or worsened?" The responses are summarized in Table 13. They may be viewed as self-assessed economic

[57]

Table 13[41]

Workers' Assessments of Recent Economic Trends

"In the past five years, has your economic situation improved, remained the same, or worsened?"

Sample	Sample Size	"Improved" Per Cent	"Remained the same" Per Cent	"Worsened" Per Cent
Santiago and Lima				
pobladores (all men)				
Santo Domingo (Santiago)	(191)	52	21	27
3 de Mayo (Santiago)	(98)	46	24	28
Pampa Seca (Lima)	(127)	33	16	51
El Espiritu (Lima)	(119)	33	13	53
Caracas *rancho* residents				
(80% women)	(258)	23	42	32
Rio *favelados*				
men and women	(200)	18	28	55
men only	(150)	21	30	48
women only	(50)	10	24	66
All-India urban samples:				
(men and women)				
1952-1957				
unskilled workers	(217)	9	39	48
skilled workers	(247)	16	44	37
income less than Rs. 100 a month	(1691)	14	41	43
1957-1959				
unskilled workers	(130)	8	43	37
skilled workers	(124)	20	37	38
income less than Rs. 100 a month	(452)	11	44	36
1962-1965				
income less than Rs. 75 a month	(49)	16	16	64
income Rs. 76-150 a month	(192)	15	35	49

Table 14[42]

Workers' Assessments of Economic Prospects

"During the next five years, do you expect your economic situation
to improve, stay the same, or become worse?"

Sample	Sample Size	"Improve" Per Cent	"Remain the same" Per Cent	"Worsen" Per Cent
Caracas *rancho* residents	(258)	69	6	7
Santiago and Lima *pobladores*				
(Santiago)	(191)	66	15	16
3 de Mayo (Santiago)	(98)	68	17	13
Pampa Seca (Lima)	(127)	32	12	50
El Espiritu (Lima)	(119)	47	17	36
Mexican working class sample	(216)	70	21	9
unskilled workers		60	27	13
skilled workers		73	19	8
men		80	12	8
women		63	27	10

mobility. In only one sub-sample—residents of the public housing project of Santo Domingo in Santiago, Chile—did more than
half of the respondents report improvement. Conversely, with
the exception of the two neighborhoods in Santiago, the proportion of those who report deterioration never falls below one-
third, and rises as high as two-thirds in major Indian metropolitan centers during a period of drought and high prices.

Despite this poor showing, surveys indicate great optimism
regarding the future — in several cases, among the same groups
reporting that economic conditions have been deteriorating in
the recent past.

Surveys also show that these and other lower class groups
believe their societies and economies are quite open, and prospects for their children are better than for themselves. Asked
whether a child from the *favela* could become the owner of a
large business, a lawyer, a university professor, a high government official, or a member of the Chamber of Deputies, 54 per
cent to 73 per cent of the male *favelados* in Bonilla's Rio sample
replied, "Yes." Women were substantially less optimistic; their

affirmative responses ran a steady twenty points below the men's replies on each item.[43]

Similarly, Caracas *rancho* residents were asked whether any capable Venezuelan could become the owner of a small or large enterprise, a lawyer, a high official, army officer, or politician. Replies ranged from 80 to 90 per cent affirmative. Ninety-two per cent of the sample believed anyone could become an office worker. Eighty-seven per cent felt that their children's opportunities would exceed their own. These responses are more striking in view of the fact that almost 80 per cent of the *rancho* sample were women.[44]

Goldrich's four samples of male *pobladores* were asked, "Do you think that when your children grow up they will have a better life than you now have?" In Lima, 90 per cent expected somewhat or much better prospects for their children than for themselves. In Santiago, 98 per cent expected a better life for their children.[45] A different, somewhat loaded question drew a

Table 15[46]

Workers' Assessments of their Children's Prospects

"What opportunity does a child of this area have to attain the position he deserves in society?"

Settlement	"Good" or "very good" Per Cent	"Little" Per Cent	"None" Per Cent
Santo Domingo (Santiago)	33	51	14
3 the Mayo (Santiago)	23	60	15
Pampa Seca (Lima)	28	61	10
El Espiritu (Lima)	20	48	29

less sanguine response.

In the Inkeles surveys, workers were asked whether a man born into a poor family could get ahead if he were ambitious and hard-working. In Argentina, Chile, India, and Pakistan, overwhelming majorities in all skill and occupational categories replied that such a man probably or surely would succeed. Table 16 shows only those who replied that the poor but industrious and ambitious man would *surely* succeed. On the basis of survey data drawn from working class neighborhoods in Buenos Aires in 1960, Gino Germani confirms the impression of optimism: "After ten years of economic stagnation and a decreasing level of

[60]

living, most of the urban proletariat still believed in success through hard work and personal initiative."[47]

Table 16[48]

Workers' Assessments of Hardworking Poor Man's Prospects

"Some say that a man born into a poor family will not get ahead even if he is ambitious and hard working. Do you think such a man will surely fail, probably fail, could well succeed, or will surely succeed?"

(Per cent saying "will *surely* succeed")

Skill/Occupation	Argentina	Chile	India	Pakistan
Unskilled factory worker	28	31	53	60
Semi-skilled factory worker	33	23	58	68
Skilled factory worker	37	28	64	71
Low-level non-factory worker	50	28	56	75
Higher-level non-factory worker	26	46	47	—
Sample size	(715)	(809)	(918)	(744)

Some of these questions may elicit optimistic responses because of their speculative nature. The question regarding economic expectations for the next five years, while concrete, may conceivably permit confusion between what is hoped for and what is expected. Even allowing for some optimistic bias, however, the pattern which emerges from opinion surveys is one of widespread dissatisfaction with economic conditions and recent trends, coupled with considerable optimism and a substantial degree of faith in the openness of the system. The assumption that large numbers of the urban poor feel frustration and acute resentment over objectively appalling conditions must be modified accordingly. Ted Gurr, discussing frustration-aggression models and their political relevance, remarks:

> Formulations of frustration in terms of the "want-get ratio," which refers only to a discrepancy between sought values and actual attainment, are too simplistic. Man lives mentally in the near future as much as in the present.[49]

Faith in the future may make present deprivation less bitter. And even if one judges one's personal prospects as bleak, belief that the system is open may dull the edge of resentment. The myth of open opportunity prevents conversion of individual misfortune into social injustice. Many of the urban poor undoubtedly are discontented, but it is not clear that their dissatisfaction is the cumulative, driving resentment postulated in the model.

Venting Frustration through Political Channels. To the extent that frustration and resentment do rise and spread, there remains the question of their transformation into political behavior in general, and politically motivated violence or radicalism in particular. As noted earlier, frustration may find expression through many channels, individual or collective, pacific or aggressive, apolitical or political. The patterns it assumes will vary among different national cultures and social groups, but everywhere and within all groups much frustration will be diverted into non-political forms.

Moreover, resort to political modes of expression and action is less likely among the poor and ill-educated than among more advantaged groups. Among the findings of survey research, few are more consistent across different studies and in different countries than the relationship between level of education (or, more generally, socio-economic status) and degree of interest, sense of efficacy, and extent of actual participation in political and public affairs. This has been demonstrated repeatedly in studies of developed countries. Almond and Verba found the same pattern in each of the five nations included in their survey: the United States, Great Britain, Germany, Italy, and Mexico. Respondents with little or no education were consistently and substantially less likely to regard government as relevant to their daily lives, to pay attention to political affairs, to discuss politics, or to become emotionally involved in electoral campaigns, that is, to feel satisfaction in voting or annoyance with politicians' speeches.[50] Respondents' belief that they could bring some influence to bear on unjust local regulations also appeared closely linked to education and level of occupation.[51] Surveys conducted by the Indian Institute of Public Opinion have asked similar or identical questions, and have elicited parallel responses. Very few among the uneducated and unskilled polled in Indian cities reported an interest in politics, claimed to care who wins national elections, believed that they could do anything to influence an unjust act on the part of local or national authorities, or stated that they had actually tried to affect a local governmental decision.[52] The CENDES surveys in Ven-

[62]

ezuela inquired into interest in politics: almost 80 per cent of the Caracas *rancho* residents polled reported that they had not talked about politics with friends in the past six months, although the survey was taken shortly before a major national election. (Electoral tensions may have caused some to hide their interests or activities, but it seems unlikely that this would swamp the elections' impact in heightening interests among the usually apathetic). An equal proportion of *favelados* in the Rio sample denied discussing politics *heatedly* with friends or acquaintances in the past half-year; presumably a higher ratio engaged in casual political conversation.[53]

There are many reasons for political apathy among the poor and ill-educated, including preoccupation with daily problems and a usually well-founded belief that the authorities are particularly unresponsive to those in their position. Many of the poor may also fail to perceive the connection between government policies and programs and the general economic conditions which perpetuate their poverty. Wealthier and better educated groups may think in terms of governmental policies and their effect on economic conditions, but marginals are less likely to trace the causes of unemployment, scarcities, or inflation to governmental action or inaction. The point is neatly documented by a set of questions asked of a large urban sample in India in 1965. Respondents were asked whether they had felt a scarcity of grain, cloth, housing, and several other commodities and services during the past few years. Those replying affirmatively were asked to whom or what they attributed responsibility for the shortages. Partial results are shown in Table 17. The patterns of blame for shortages of cloth, housing, and education were similar to that for foodgrains. In every case the proportion attributing responsibility to the government is lowest among the poorest and least educated groups, and rises sharply among groups one step higher in the hierarchy. It seems fair to assume that groups less prone to blame the government for shortages are also less likely to regard political activity as an effective means of alleviating shortages.

Proponents of the radicalization theory might fairly protest at this point that evidence of low political awareness and participation among the urban poor is largely irrelevant to their argument. The theory does not assert that marginals are participant

[63]

Table 17[54]

Socio-economic Status and Tendency to Blame Government for Shortages
"To whose policy do you ascribe this shortfall (in foodgrains)?"

	Number reporting scarcity	Per cent blaming gov't	Per cent blaming others	Per cent blaming both
Income Group				
Under Rs. 75	(30)	30	23	30
76-150	(142)	58	12	32
151-300	(182)	59	9	31
301-500	(67)	58	6	30
Education				
Illiterate and literate but without formal education	(56)	37	7	30
Primary, under-matric and matric	(229)	49	8	35
Some college	(270)	59	8	28
Occupation				
Worker	(38)	42	16	34
Salaried employee	(265)	57	9	26
Independent	(163)	60	8	30

and radical initially or inherently. Rather, it predicts that they will become more so as the proportion of marginals with long urban experience grows. The second-generation variant suggests that participation and radicalism will increase with the rising ratio of urban-born to migrants among the marginal population. Both theories predict trends, and cannot be disproved by describing contrary conditions at any particular point in time.

True enough. But neither theory spells out clearly the mechanism which produces the predicted trend. What are the influences causing significant numbers of marginals to shift their outlook from apathetic disinterest to participant radicalism?

Simply living in the city is not enough. The careful and extensive analyses of Inkeles and his associates demonstrate that urban residence adds little to the explanation of differences in politicization and political participation among groups matched for level of education, length of factory experience, age, and other factors.[55] The length of urban residence is much less important in remolding attitudes and behavior than the range and intensity of influences bearing on the individual, among which education and occupation are two of the most important. Consider a young man who comes to the city at fifteen, gains one or two years of vocational education, and finds a job as a semi-skilled mechanic's assistant in a modern and unionized factory. Compare him with an illiterate woman who comes to the city with her husband, holds no job other than taking in occasional washing, and lives in a squatter settlement where she associates primarily with relatives and almost never ventures into the city around her. The young man will have more exposure to urban influences in three or four years than the woman will have in the same number of decades.

There is, of course, an association between length of urban residence and exposure to urban influences. *But the essence of marginality is failure to gain access, hence exposure, to urban institutions and processes:* education, adequate employment, services, housing, consumer goods, social status and contacts, organizational membership, political influence. To the extent that men or women remain truly marginal, their contact with the politicizing agents of the city is likely to be limited.

The Inkeles studies clearly identify length of factory experience and amount of education as the two most powerful factors determining the level of participant citizenship among working class respondents.[56] To these might be added a third factor which the Inkeles surveys did not attempt to measure: activity by political parties or other explicit political agents among the groups from which the respondents are drawn. Other factors undoubtedly also contribute to or detract from politicization: among these are positive (housing, welfare services) or negative (squatter clearance) activities by government agencies.[57]

Marginality was defined, however, partly in terms of inability to find a steady factory job or its equivalent in income, security, and status. Those who do find such employment are well on their way to integration into the urban economy and society. Some may also become more politically active as a result of exposure to political influence in their places of work. However, this pattern of politicization is not at all that described by the radicalization theory; indeed, it is its opposite.

Those who remain marginal are unlikely to become politicized through their work experiences and associates. However,

[65]

political awareness and participation among urban marginals may grow with increases in the proportion of the urban poor with more than three or four years of education. The urban poor may also be encouraged to enter the political arena through the efforts of political parties seeking to mobilize their votes. In most developing countries, the established parties have campaigned in poorer parts of the cities during elections, but have made relatively little effort to develop continuing organization and sustained loyalties among the poor. Conservative elite or middle class parties view the poor as dubious allies. Even parties more ideologically disposed to organize the underprivileged may be deterred by the formidable difficulties of working among groups with few organizational ties, shifting occupations, high residential turnover, limited internal leadership, intense suspicions against outsiders, substantial mistrust even within their own circles, and low initial levels of political interest or awareness. The political isolation of marginal groups is partially self-perpetuating: they do not participate because they have few ties to the political processes of the nation; but established political groups hesitate to try to organize the poor, in part because of their low levels of politicization.

The circle can be and is being broken—gradually but steadily by the extension of educational opportunities to poorer urban neighborhoods, and less predictably but more dramatically by the efforts of new or revitalized or reoriented parties. The extent to which schools are available to and parties are active among the urban poor varies greatly from country to country, and changes over time within individual nations. Moreover, the spread of schools and party activity among the poor is determined by factors which are not included in the framework of the radicalization theories, that is, by decisions taken in governmental ministries and party councils.

4. Conclusions

As a predictive instrument, the theory of radicalization and the deprivation-frustration-aggression model on which it rests are misleading. The theory itself does not specify the pace of radicalization. But it is usually linked to predictions of political upheaval in the not too distant future. Such calculations probably exaggerate the rate at which the aspirations of the poor rise, and underestimate the incidence of modest but psychologically important progress. Therefore, proponents of the theory overstate the rate at which discontent spreads among the urban lower classes. Their calculations also imply a high rate of conversion from frustration to radical political action. In fact, the bulk of economic and social frustration is likely to leak into alternative channels, including non-radical political action.

As an analytic framework, the radicalization theory is also seriously deficient. Since the poor virtually everywhere have little interest in and awareness of politics, a theory which predicts that they will come to play an active and disruptive role must explain how their attitudes and behavior are to be transformed. The radicalization theory merely assumes, without explaining, the process of politicization. I have already argued that not all frustration leads to political activity. It is also true that not all political activity among the urban poor is an expression of frustration. Individuals have many motives for taking part in political activity. Desire for sociability or for enhanced status, loyalty to friends, or the search for entertainment and excitement, as well as frustration, may lead to political participation.

Moreover, the form of political activity is powerfully shaped by the nation's political culture and the specific political context, which should be viewed as independent of (though interacting with) the motivations underlying political involvement. The dispersion and content of education and mass media, political party activity among the urban poor, and in some cases church and local neighborhood organizations all affect the direction of political activity. All of these variables are exogenous to the deprivation-frustration-aggression model.

While the theory of the disruptive migrants is demonstrably wrong, the theory of the radical marginals may be valid under some conditions. The problem is that the theory itself contributes very little toward identifying those conditions. In short, although the radicalization theory points to processes and tendencies which are indeed important, it is too incomplete and loosely articulated a theory to be valuable, either for prediction or as a framework for research.

[67]

A Prospectus

The theory of the disruptive migrants and the theory of the radical marginals share three serious flaws. Both stress social psychology to the point of ignoring crucial political variables. Both fail to distinguish important differences within the large and heterogeneous population groups with which they are concerned. As a result, both produce rather narrow and dubious predictions, rather than exploring the possible range of political roles which migrants and the urban poor may play under various circumstances.

The shared flaws may have common origins. Fear of the urban mob is as ancient as cities. Concern about rapid migration and resulting urban growth was widespread in Europe during the nineteenth century and earlier: that is, as the movement of people off the land accelerated. Foreign scholars observing today's developing nations are not immune to similar preconceptions. Moreover, North American observers are understandably tempted to draw analogies between recent unrest in urban ghettoes of the United States and apparently similar or worse conditions in low-income urban neighborhoods abroad.

A broader set of questions and a more comprehensive framework of analysis are needed. The question of destabilization or radicalization has pre-empted much of the meager attention scholars have given to the study of the political implications of urban growth abroad. Yet if we want to locate the sources of urban turbulence and extremism, recent migrants and the urban poor are the wrong groups to examine. This is not to argue that there are no conditions under which they could become disruptive, but rather that other groups have been much more important in disturbances to date. If, however, we are interested in the current and potential political role of migrants and the poor, preoccupation with instability blinds us to a number of more probable, and equally interesting patterns of evolution.

An exploration of possible patterns of political integration or disintegration should proceed at three levels. At the level of individuals, we need to know much more about the experiences which heighten political awareness, the perceptions which create a sense of legitimacy or alienation, and the motivations which spur men to engage in political action. This level of inquiry must rely heavily on attitude survey techniques, perhaps supplemented with intensive studies of neighborhoods or communities.

To gauge the likelihood of collective action, we need information not only on the forces that alter individual attitudes and behavior, but also on the incidence of such influences within the population group that interests us. What is the educational profile of urban marginal populations in particular countries or cities? Assuming some knowledge of the politicizing influences associated with various types of occupations, what is the occupational distribution of the marginal population? If experience with local neighborhood organizations is found to shape individual political attitudes, what is the incidence of such organizations in poor neighborhoods? If certain kinds of experience connected with squatting tend to influence political views, what proportion of the urban poor are squatters? How do these various influences combine to reinforce or dilute each others' force?

These are static questions. However, if we are interested in prediction, we must also ask whether, and how rapidly, the most important politicizing forces are extending their impact among the urban poor. Trends are both absolute and relative. The number of poor children completing elementary school may be rising steadily, but the proportion of school-age children finishing the first level of education may rise, fall, or remain constant, depending on demographic factors of natural population increase and in-migration. Moreover, trends are qualitative as well as quantitative. Not only may the proportion of migrants from rural areas shift, but their average education and skill level and the nature of their political experience in the countryside may also change.

In order to understand both the extent to which the agents and channels of political socialization impinge upon the urban poor, and the rate and direction of change in politicizing forces, analysts must look beyond the immediate environment of the urban poor to the broader political and social context. Under what conditions, for example, do established political parties undertake an active and sustained campaign to mobilize urban marginals? Such a course would appear most likely where elections are important in the national political system, party competition is substantial, and at least one major party is ideologically or strategically disposed to seek mass support. Alternatively, where middle class groups face an unyielding traditional elite, they may seek an alliance with the urban poor. Such hypotheses can best be tested through a broad comparative approach.

Explanations of the current political role of urban marginals and predictions of their potential roles under various circumstances must be based on understanding of the causes of individual differences in political attitudes and behavior, the incidence of politicizing forces among the urban poor, and the interplay between the broader social, economic, and political context and the agents and channels of political socialization. The three levels of analysis call for different methods of research and different types of data. Each is interesting in its own right. Each, however, is incomplete without the other elements. All are essential for a full-fledged theory of political integration of the urban poor.

1. In Brazil and Mexico between 1940 and 1950, population in cities of 100,000 or more grew at average annual rates of 5 and 6.7 per cent respectively. During the 1950's, Santo Domingo grew 7.3 per cent yearly; Panama City expanded at a rate of 7.9 per cent. (United Nations, *Compendium of Social Statistics*, 1963, Series K, No. 2, Table 7.) In the 1950's and early 1960's, Bogotá's population rose an average of 6.8 per cent a year; Cali's increased at 6.3 per cent. (Paul T. Schultz, "Population and Labor Force Projections for Colombia, 1964-1974," mimeo., Santa Monica, California, RAND, July 10, 1967, p. 12.) Between 1941 and 1959 Caracas averaged 7.4 per cent annual growth. (Bruce Herrick, *Urban Migration and Economic Development in Chile* (Cambridge, Mass.: M.I.T. Press, 1965), p. 31.) And in some parts of Asia and the Near East, rapid urban growth rivals that of Latin America. Korean cities have been growing rapidly since the 1950's: Seoul added 6.6 per cent more people each year from 1960 to 1966. Turkey's population centers of 100,000 or more grew 6.7 per cent a year from 1955 to 1960; Ankara averaged 6.8 per cent annually from 1960 to 1965. (Estimated from figures in United Nations, *Demographic Yearbook*, 1962, 1963, 1967.) In South Asia, urban growth rates are generally lower. Delhi grew 5 per cent a year from 1951 to 1961, but greater Bombay expanded at an annual rate of 3.9 per cent during that period, and Calcutta's rate was 1.9 per cent, reflecting in part the immense size already reached by these two giants. (Kingsley Davis in Roy Turner, ed., *India's Urban Future* (Berkeley: University of California Press, 1962), p. 10.)
2. See, for example, Ivo K. and Rosalind L. Feierabend, "Aggressive Behaviors Within Polities: 1948-1962: A Cross-National Study," *Journal of Conflict Resolution*, 10:3 (September 1966), pp. 249-271; Douglas Bwy, "Political Instability in Latin America: The Cross-cultural Test of a Causal Model," *Latin American Research Review*, 3:2 (Spring 1968), pp. 17-66.
3. An outstanding exception is James Payne, *Labor and Politics in Peru* (New Haven: Yale University Press, 1965).
4. Labor in developing countries is poorly trained and unreliable. Moreover, many countries have social security laws which are enforced primarily or solely in larger manufacturing enterprises. As a result, labor costs per unit of output may be quite high despite low hourly or daily wages. Furthermore, development policies such as rapid write-off and other tax concessions and special exchange rates for imported capital equipment reduce the cost of capital compared to labor. From the entrepreneur's standpoint, labor may be relatively costly and capital comparatively cheap even in countries where labor is plentiful and capital scarce.
5. A convenient collection of estimates of unemployment in developing countries may be found in Fred Dziadek, *Unemployment in the Less Developed Countries*, AID Discussion Paper No. 16, Washington, D.C.,

[71]

Agency for International Development, June 1967, Appendix A. See also Robert Slighton, *Urban Unemployment in Colombia: Measurement, Characteristics, and Policy Problems*, RAND RM 5393-AID, Santa Monica, California, RAND, January 1968, p. 16 and passim (Bogotá); W. F. Maunder, *Employment in an Underdeveloped Area: A Sample Survey of Kingston, Jamaica* (New Haven: Yale University Press, 1960), pp. 157-158; N. V. Sovani, *Urbanization and Urban India* (Bombay: Asia Publishing House, 1966), pp. 154-155 (six Indian cities); V.K.R.V. Rao and P. B. Desai, *Greater Delhi: A Study in Urbanization 1940-1957* (New York: Asia Publishing House, 1965), pp. 379 ff; P. C. Malhotra, *Socio-economic Survey of Bhopal City and Bairagahr* (New York: Asia Publishing House, 1964), pp. 93 ff; S. Hashmi *et al.*, *The People of Karachi: Data from a Survey* (Karachi: Institute of Development Economics, 1964), pp. 112 ff. The Economic Commission for Asia and the Far East (ECAFE) has estimated open urban unemployment in India, Japan, Thailand, and the Federation of Malaya as 2 to 2.5 per cent of the urban labor force, but this estimate uses the Indian census definition of "urban" as any population center of over 2,000 persons. (ECAFE, "Population Growth and Problems of Employment," *Economic Bulletin for Asia and the Far East*, 12:2 (1961), p. 11.)

6. Dziadek, *op. cit.*, p. A-2.
7. Hollis B. Chenery, *Toward a More Effective Alliance for Progress*, AID Discussion Paper No. 13, Washington, D.C., Agency for International Development, 1967, p. 12.
8. Werner Baer and Michel Herve, "Employment and Industrialization in Developing Countries," *Quarterly Journal of Economics*, 80 (February 1966), p. 89; Economic Commission for Latin America (ECLA), "Structural Changes in Employment within the Context of Latin America's Economic Development," *Economic Bulletin for Latin America*, 10:2 (October 1965), p. 176. For a critique of the concept of over-urbanization and a more balanced discussion of the benefits and drawbacks of rapid urban growth, see N. V. Sovani, "The Analysis of Over-Urbanization," *Economic Development and Cultural Change*, 12:2 (1964), pp. 113-122, and John Friedmann and Tomás Lackington, "Hyperurbanization and National Development in Chile," *Urban Affairs Quarterly*, 2:4 (1967), pp. 3-29.
9. Not all squatters, however, are marginal in the economic, social, and political senses. Construction of conventional housing has lagged so far behind urban population growth that for many of the less affluent, squatting and self-help construction have become the only feasible means of acquiring adequate housing. Estimates place a fifth to a quarter of Lima's population in the early 1960's in squatter settlements; 16 per cent of Rio's as of 1964; 30 per cent of Caracas' in the late 1950's (despite construction of immense public housing projects absorbing an additional 18 per cent of the city's population); and over a third of Mexico City. (Richard M. Morse, "Recent Research on Latin American Urbanization," *Latin American Research Review*, 1:1 (1965), p. 50;

John F. C. Turner, "Uncontrolled Urban Settlement: Problems and Policies," mimeo., prepared for the Interregional Seminar on Development Policies and Planning in Relation to Urbanization, organized by the U.N. Bureau of Technical Assistance Operations and the Bureau of Social Affairs, 1966, p. 1.) In Turkey, Granville Sewell estimates that squatters comprise a fifth of Istanbul, a third of Ankara, and a third of Adana. ("Squatter Settlements in Turkey," unpublished doctoral dissertation, Cambridge, Mass., M.I.T., 1964, pp. 71, 186, 193.) Some of these extensive settlements are slums, but many are incipient working class neighborhoods, and some are already well established blue-collar and lower middle class communities.

10. Peter Lupsha's interesting article, "On Theories of Urban Violence," presented at the American Political Science Association meetings in 1968, lists many more theories of the causes of urban violence, including "conspiracy," "riff-raff," "teen-age rebellion," and "police brutality." However, the "recent migrant" and "frustration-aggression" theories discussed here are the two theories which appear most often in discussions of urban problems in the developing nations.

1. Barbara Ward, "The Uses of Prosperity," *Saturday Review*, August 29, 1964, pp. 191-192, cited in Myron Weiner, "Urbanization and Political Protest," *Civilisations*, 17:2 (1967), pp. 1-2; also in John Turner, "Uncontrolled Urban Settlement: Problems and Policies," p. 51, and Talton Ray, *The Politics of the Barrios of Venezuela* (Berkeley: University of California Press, 1969), p. 159.

2. Frantz Fanon, *The Wretched of the Earth*, translated from the French by Constance Farrington (London: MacGibbon and Kee, 1965), p. 103. (Copyright © 1963 by *Présence Africaine*, published by Grove Press, Inc.)

3. "Migrants" are defined as persons born outside of the city where they are currently living. Later in the chapter I distinguish between "new migrants" and "established migrants." The length of residence in the city taken as a dividing line is clearly arbitrary, and may vary according to the purpose for which the division is made and according to the form in which data are available.

4. Bertram Hutchinson, "The Migrant Population of Urban Brazil," *America Latina*, 6:2 (1963), pp. 43, 46.

5. Paul Schultz, *Population and Labor Force Projections for Colombia, 1964-1974*, p. 2.

6. Philip Hauser, "The Social, Economic, and Technological Problems of Rapid Urbanization," in Bert F. Hoselitz and Wilbert E. Moore, eds., *Industrialization and Society* (The Hague: Mouton, 1963), pp. 210-211, quoted in James Tilly and James Rule, *Measuring Political Upheaval*, Research Monograph No. 19, Center of International Studies, Princeton University, 1965, p. 16.

7. Glaucio Soares and Robert L. Hamblin, "Socio-economic Variables and Voting for the Radical Left; Chile, 1952," *American Political Science Review*, 61:4 (1967), p. 1055. See also Mancur Olson, "Economic Growth as a Destabilizing Force," *Journal of Economic History*, 23:4 (1963), p. 534.

8. Weiner, *op. cit.*, pp. 4-5.

9. Soares and Hamblin, *op. cit.*, p. 1062.

10. National Advisory Commission on Civil Disorders, *Report*, advance edition printed by the *New York Times* Company, 1968, pp. 130-131.

11. Peter Lupsha, "On Theories of Urban Violence," p. 7.

12. Charles Tilly, "Urbanization and Political Disturbances in Nineteenth Century France," mimeo., presented to the annual meeting of the Society for French Historical Studies, Ann Arbor, Michigan, April 1966, p. 6.

13. *Ibid.*, pp. 7-8.

14. *Ibid.*

15. Bruce Herrick, *Urban Migration and Economic Development in Chile*, pp. 53, 103.

16. Hutchinson, *op. cit.*, pp. 43-44.

17. D. T. Lakdawala, *Work, Wages, and Well-being in an Indian Metropo-*

lis: Economic Surveys of Bombay City (Bombay: University of Bombay, 1963), p. 159.

18. V. K. R. V. Rao and P. B. Desai, *Greater Delhi: A Study in Urbanization, 1940-1957*, p. 79.
19. William L. Flinn, "Rural-to-Urban Migration: A Colombian Case," mimeo., Research Publication No. 19, Land Tenure Center, University of Wisconsin, July 1966, pp. 10, 23.
20. Granville Sewell, "Squatter Settlements in Turkey," p. 304.
21. Herrick, *op. cit.*, p. 49.
22. Oscar Lewis, "Urbanization without Breakdown," *Scientific Monthly*, 75 (July 1952), p. 39; Lakdawala, *op. cit.*, pp. 173-174.
23. Mario Margulis, "Estudio de las Migraciones en su Lugar de Origen," *America Latina*, 9:4 (1966).
24. Sewell, *op. cit.*, p. 38.
25. Anthony and Elizabeth Leeds, "Brazil and the Myth of Urban Rurality: Urban Experience, Work, and Values in 'Squatments' of Rio de Janeiro and Lima," mimeo., prepared for the Conference on Urbanization and Work in Modernizing Societies, St. Thomas, V.I., November 1967, p. 6 and passim.
26. Marshall Wolfe, "Rural Settlement Patterns and Social Change in Latin America: Notes for a Strategy of Rural Development," *Latin American Research Review*, 1:2 (1966), p. 25.
27. Gino Germani, "Inquiry into the Social Effects of Urbanization in a Working Class Sector of Greater Buenos Aires," United Nations Economic and Social Council, E/CN.12/URB/10, December 1958, pp. 58-62.
28. *Ibid*, Table 10, p. 26.
29. Herrick, *op. cit.*, p. 91, and ECLA, "Urbanization in Latin America: Results of a Field Survey of Living Conditions in an Urban Sector," mimeo., E/CN.12.622, 1963, p. 17.
30. Flinn, *op. cit.*, p. 27.
31. Hutchinson, *op. cit.*, Table 12, p. 61.
32. William Mangin, "The Role of Regional Associations in the Adaption of Rural Migrants to Cities in Peru," in Dwight Heath and Richard Adams, eds., *Contemporary Cultures and Societies of Latin America* (New York: Random House, 1965), p. 319.
33. Herrick, *op. cit.*, p. 99.
34. Richard Patch, "Life in a Callejon: A Study of Urban Disorganization," American Universities Field Staff *Reports*, West Coast South America Series, 8:6 (1961).
35. William Mangin and Jerome Cohen, "Cultural and Psychological Characteristics of Mountain Migrants to Lima," *Sociologus*, 14:1 (1965), pp. 81-88.
36. If many migrants do have jobs in view before they move, cityward migration may be self-regulating to some degree, responding rather quickly to changes in employment prospects. The possibility deserves to be explored, but falls outside the scope of this study.

[75]

37. Herrick, *op. cit.*, p. 92.
38. ECLA, "Results of a Field Survey . . . ," *op. cit.*, p. 16.
39. Germani, *op. cit.*, Table 37, p. 69.
40. Hutchinson, *op. cit.*, pp. 67-68.
41. Robert Slighton, *Urban Unemployment in Colombia: Measurement, Characteristics, and Policy Problems*, p. 38.
42. Herrick, *op. cit.*, p. 84.
43. Weiner, *op. cit.*, p. 6.
44. Rao and Desai, *op. cit.*, Table 16-1, p. 341, and Table 17-3, p. 383.
45. Lakdawala, *op. cit.*, p. 481.
46. R. Mukerjee and B. Singh, *Social Profiles of a Metropolis* (Bombay: Asia Publishing House, 1961), p. 116.
47. G. M. Farooq, *The People of Karachi: Economic Characteristics*, Monographs in the Economics of Development No. 15, Karachi, Pakistan, Institute of Development Economics, July 1966, p. 19.
48. Germani, *op. cit.*, Table 29, p. 51.
49. Rao and Desai, *op. cit.*, Table 16-19, p. 373.
50. Herrick, *op. cit.*, Table 6-9, p. 86.
51. *Ibid.*, p. 87; Lakdawala, *op. cit.*, Table VI-37, Columns 7-8, p. 466.
52. Mukerjee and Singh, *op. cit.*, pp. 88-89.
53. Rao and Desai, *op. cit.*, Table 12-15, p. 223.
54. Herrick, *op. cit.*, p. 79; Slighton, *op. cit.*, p. 37.
55. Rao and Desai, *op. cit.*, Tables 5-14, 5-15, pp. 94-95.
56. Herrick, *op. cit.*, pp. 94-95.
57. Calculated from Hutchinson, *op. cit.*, Table 1, p. 49, by excluding urban-born and foreign immigrants from the base figures. Further data in Table 2, p. 51.
58. Germani, *op. cit.*, Table 31, p. 55; p. 56.
59. Hutchinson, *op. cit.*, p. 70.
60. J. R. Brandão Lopes, "Aspects of the Adjustment of Rural Migrants to Urban Industrial Conditions in São Paulo, Brazil," in Hauser, *op. cit.*, p. 240; Joseph A. Kahl, "Three Types of Mexican Industrial Workers," *Economic Development and Cultural Change*, 8:2 (1960), p. 165.
61. Guillermo Briones, "Mobilidad Occupacional y Mercado de Trabajo en el Peru," *America Latina*, 6:3 (1963), pp. 70-71.
62. Germani, *op. cit.*, p. 16.
63. Andrew Pearse, "Some Characteristics of Urbanization in the City of Rio de Janeiro," in Philip Hauser, ed., *Urbanization in Latin America* (Paris: UNESCO, 1961), p. 196.
69. Frank Bonilla, "Rio's Favelas; The Rural Slum Within the City," American Universities Field Staff *Reports*, East Coast South America Series, 8:3 (1961), p. 2.
65. Pearse, *op. cit.*
66. Doris Phillips, "Rural-to-Urban Migration in Iraq," *Economic Development and Cultural Change*, 7:4 (July 1959), p. 417.

[76]

67. *Ibid.*
68. Flinn, *op. cit.*, pp. 5, 37.
69. Sewell, *op. cit.*, pp. 109-110.
70. Janet Abu-Lughod, "Urbanization in Egypt: Present State and Future Prospects," *Economic Development and Cultural Change,* 13:3 (1965), p. 315.
71. Sewell, *op. cit.*, p. 91.
72. See, for example, Richard Patch's account of one such migrant, in "La Parada, Lima's Market, Part I: A Villager Who Met Disaster," American Universities Field Staff *Reports,* West Coast South America Series, 14:1, (1967).
73. Weiner, *op. cit.*, p. 6.
74. Until very recently the level of development in Southern Italy, as measured by average income, proportion of labor force engaged in agriculture, proportions of artisans within the labor force engaged in manufacturing, average levels of education, and per cent of school age children in school, was roughly comparable to many of the countries of Latin America.
75. Robert C. Fried, "Urbanization and Italian Politics," *Journal of Politics,* 29:3 (1967), pp. 529-530.
76. *Ibid.,* p. 523.
77. *Ibid.,* pp. 527-528.
78. *Ibid.,* p. 513.
79. *Ibid.,* p. 516.
80. *Ibid.,* p. 520.
81. *Ibid.,* p. 523.
82. *Ibid.,* p. 521.
83. *Ibid.*
84. *Ibid.,* pp. 522-523.
85. *Ibid.,* p. 525.
86. *Ibid.,* pp. 526-527.

1. Kingsley Davis and Hilda H. Golden, "Urbanization and the Development of Pre-industrial Areas," *Economic Development and Cultural Change*, 3:1 (1954), pp. 19-20.
2. Glaucio Soares, "The Political Sociology of Uneven Development in Brazil," in Irving L. Horowitz, ed., *Revolution in Brazil* (New York: Dutton, 1964), pp. 192, 195.
3. Adam Ulam, *The Unfinished Revolution* (New York: Random House, 1960), p. 60.
4. *Ibid.*
5. Talton Ray, *The Politics of the Barrios of Venezuela* (MS), pp. 281-282.
6. Granville Sewell, "Squatter Settlements in Turkey," pp. 204-205.
7. Samuel P. Huntington, *Political Order in Changing Societies* (New Haven: Yale University Press, 1968), pp. 281-283.
8. Daniel Goldrich *et al.*, "The Political Integration of Lower Class Urban Settlements," mimeo., prepared for the American Political Science Association meetings, September 1966, p. 19.
9. ECLA, "Geographic Distribution of the Population of Latin America and Regional Development Priorities," UN Document E/CN.12/643 (February 1963), pp. 5-8; cited in Morse, "Recent Research on Latin American Urbanization," p. 51.
10. In Latin America, the average annual rate of growth of agricultural employment has remained at a steady 1.3-1.4 per cent since 1925. (ECLA, "Structural Changes in Employment within the Context of Latin America's Economic Development," *Economic Bulletin for Latin America*, 10:2 (October 1965), p. 165.)
11. Calculated from data in Economic Commission for Asia and the Far East, "Population Growth and Problems of Employment in the ECAFE Region," *Economic Bulletin for Asia and the Far East*, 12:2 (September 1961), Table 14, p. 18.
12. ECLA, *op. cit.*, p. 167.
13. *Ibid.*, p. 166.
14. It is more complicated but more accurate to define "new migrants" as those with less than a stated number of years of residence in *any* city over a specified size, excluding urban residence while very young.
15. See Maurice Zeitlin, *Revolutionary Politics and the Cuban Working Class* (Princeton, New Jersey: Princeton University Press, 1967), Chapter 9.
16. Soares, *op. cit.*, p. 192.
17. Gabriel Almond and Sidney Verba, *The Civic Culture* (Princeton, New Jersey: Princeton University Press, 1963), Appendix A, p. 514.
18. Daniel Goldrich, "Partisanship and Political Integration," mimeo. draft manuscript dated August 1967, Table 5, p. 14-A.
19. Indian Institute of Public Opinion, "The Structure of Urban Public Opinion," *Public Opinion Surveys*, 11:5, No. 125 (February 1966), pp. 15-16.

20. Indian Institute of Public Opinion, "An All-India Survey of Urban Political Opinion," *Public Opinion Surveys*, 10, No. 114 (March 1965), p. 7.

21. George F. Jones, "Urbanization and Voting Behavior in Venezuela and Chile, 1958-1964," typescript prepared at Stanford University, March 1967, pp. 40-43.

22. *Ibid.*, pp. 69-72.

23. Myron Weiner, "Violence and Politics in Calcutta," *The Journal of Asian Studies*, 20:3 (1961), p. 277.

24. Charles Tilly, "A Travers le Chaos des Vivantes Cités," mimeo. paper presented to the Sixth World Congress of Sociology, Evian-les-Bains, September 1966, pp. 17, 19.

25. The Inkeles survey also included Israel and Nigeria. I have omitted Israel because the entire sample is of urban origin; Nigeria is excluded because my study as a whole does not extend to sub-Saharan Africa.

26. Andrew Whiteford, *Two Cities of Latin America: A Comparative Description of Social Classes* (New York: Anchor Books, Doubleday, 1964), p. 120.

27. Oscar Lewis, "The Culture of Poverty," *Scientific American*, October 1966, p. 21.

28. Suzanne Keller and Marisa Zavalloni, "Ambition and Social Class," *Social Forces*, 43 (October 1964), pp. 61-62.

29. Whiteford, *op. cit.*, p. 120.

30. S. Michael Miller and Frank Reisman, "The Working Class Subculture," *Social Problems*, 9 (Summer 1961), pp. 92, 95-96.

31. Herbert J. Gans, *The Urban Villagers* (New York: The Free Press, 1962), pp. 219-221, and passim.

32. Sources for data in Table 13: *São Paulo:* Bertram Hutchinson's survey data as reported in S. M. Miller, "Comparative Social Mobility," *Current Sociology*, 9 (1960), p. 69. *Buenos Aires:* Gino Germani, "La Mobilidad Social en la Argentina," mimeo., Publicacion Interna No. 60, Instituto de Sociologia, Facultad de Filosofia y Letras, Universidad de Buenos Aires. *Poona:* N. V. Sovani, "Occupational Mobility in Poona Between Three Generations," in *Urbanization and Urban India* (Bombay: Asia Publishing House, 1966), p. 96.

33. Bertram Hutchinson, "Urban Social Mobility Rates in Brazil Related to Migration and Changing Occupational Structure," *America Latina*, 6:3 (1963), Table 4, p. 54.

34. Seymour Martin Lipset and Reinhard Bendix, *Social Mobility in Industrial Society* (Berkeley and Los Angeles: University of California Press, 1959), pp. 216-219.

35. Gino Germani, data developed for but not presented in the study on social mobility cited above.

36. See John F. C. Turner, "Uncontrolled Urban Settlement: Problems and Policies."

37. Goldrich, "The Political Integration of Lower Class Urban Settlements," p. 4.

[79]

38. William Flinn, "Rural-to-Urban Migration: A Colombian Case," pp. 3-4.
39. Stephan Thernstrom, *Poverty and Progress: Social Mobility in a 19th Century City* (Cambridge, Mass.: Harvard University Press, 1964), pp. 163, 165.
40. Gino Germani, "Social and Political Consequences of Mobility," in Neil Smelser and Seymour Martin Lipset, eds., *Social Structure and Mobility in Economic Development* (Chicago: Aldine, 1966), pp. 379-380.
41. Sources for Table 13. *Santiago and Lima:* Daniel Goldrich, "Politics and the *Pobladore:* Political Behavior in Four Lower Class Settlements," draft manuscript, Table 4, p. 20-A, "Morale." *Caracas:* CENDES survey data, print-out of marginals. *Rio:* Frank Bonilla, "Rio's Favelas: The Rural Slum within the City," p. 8. *All-India urban samples:* 1952-1957. Indian Institute of Public Opinion, *Public Opinion Surveys,* 2, Nos. 16-19 (January-April 1957), pp. 98-99, 1957-1959: Indian Institute of Public Opinion, *Public Opinion Surveys,* 4, Nos. 45-48 (June-September, 1959), pp. 32. 1962-1965: Indian Institute of Public Opinion, *Public Opinion Surveys,* 10, No. 114 (March 1965), p. 15.
42. Sources for Table 14. *Santiago and Lima:* Goldrich, *op. cit.,* Table 4, p. 20-A. *Caracas:* CENDES print-out. *Mexican working class:* developed from taped data of Almond and Verba "Civic Culture" survey.
43. Bonilla, *op. cit.,* p. 11.
44. CENDES print-out.
45. Goldrich, *op. cit.,* "Demographic and Socio-economic Background, Social Mobility, and Expectations," Table 1, p. 17.
46. *Ibid.*
47. Germani, *op. cit.,* pp. 389-390.
48. Developed from Inkeles survey data.
49. Ted Gurr, "Psychological Determinants of Civil Violence," *World Politics,* 20:2 (January 1968), p. 257. Gurr was discussing anticipated deprivation, but the point applies equally to expected gratification or achievement.
50. Gabriel A. Almond and Sidney Verba, *The Civic Culture,* pp. 87, 94, 121, 152.
51. *Ibid.,* pp. 206, 210.
52. Indian Institute of Public Opinion, *Public Opinion Surveys.* Regarding degree of interest in politics: vol. 2 (July 1957), vol. 4 (June 1959), vol. 7 (November 1961). Regarding whether the respondent cares who wins the 1957 elections: vol. 2 (January-April 1957), pp. 39-40. Regarding sense of efficacy and actual attempts to influence local or national authorities: vol. 12 (April-June 1967), pp. 99-104.
53. Bonilla, *op. cit.,* p. 12.
54. Derived from Indian Institute of Public Opinion, *Public Opinion Surveys,* 10, No. 114 (March 1965), pp. 21-32.

[80]

55. Alex Inkeles, "Participant Citizenship in Six Developing Countries," mimeo., draft chapter for forthcoming book, dated January 1968, p. 39.
56. *Ibid.*, p. 32.
57. Media exposure, while closely associated statistically with politicization, is hard to identify as a causal factor, since there is obviously a reciprocal relationship between political interest and radio and newspaper use.